COMMENTARIES ON
THE OCCULT
PHILOSOPHY OF
AGRIPPA

COMMENTARIES ON THE OCCULT PHILOSOPHY OF AGRIPPA

Willy Schrödter

SAMUEL WEISER, INC.

York Beach, Maine

First published in 2000 by
Samuel Weiser, Inc.
Box 612
York Beach, ME 03910-0612
www.weiserbooks.com

First hardcover edition, 2000. Translation copyright © 2000 Samuel Weiser, Inc.

Library of Congress Cataloging-in-Publication Data
Schrödter, Willy, 1897-
    [Agrippa von Netteseheim De occulta philosophia. English]
    Commentaries on the occult philosophy of Agrippa / Willy Schrödter.
        p. cm.
    Includes bibliographical references and indexes.
    ISBN 0-87728-944-1 (alk. paper)—ISBN 0-87728-922-0 (pbk. : alk. paper)
        1. Agrippa von Nettesheim, Heinrich Cornelius, 1486?–1535. De occulta philosophia. I. Title
    B781.A33 O33713 2000
    133—dc21   99–058154

EB

Translated by Transcript, Ltd

Typeset in 11/13 Palatino

Printed in the United States of America

The paper used in this publication meets all the minimum requirements of the American National Standard for Information Sciences—Permanence of Paper for Printed Library Materials Z39.48-1992 (R1997).

For my friend Herwart von Guilleaume

Willy Schröter

CONTENTS

THE ADEPT

The taper smokes. A hot drop hits my hand,
Changing from molten into solid wax.
Stiffened by age, the bending parchment cracks,
And in the circle's ambushment I stand.
Who tempted me to sweep this hidden closet,
The sorcerer's old chest to clear away?
Who ordered me to bring his dark deposit,
Abstruse, mysterious, to the light of day?

The pentagram, that high seal, flares
Metallic in the flickering zone,
And shadows lengthen . . . This black stone
I hold—untaught from whence it fares—
Scented by Eastern joss-sticks faintly,
And treasured in its gray silk binding,
Oval and glassy, for my finding,
Lay hidden in the chest so quaintly.

I found this book, and amber ring, and dirk
Stamped with the zodiac signs in burnished gold,
And—yon steel demon, goggle-eyed and bold,
A salamander watching me at work . . .
One of an upsurge of uncanny faces
Willing to trespass upon our condition . . .
O Elemental! Who gave you permission
To come and haunt us in our human places?

Ah, the old pride! Did not *I* then go
Piercing the circle to its alien heart,
Misusing what I thought I had of art,
Evoking entities I did not know?

The taper weeps. My fingers are set golden
In hardened wax where they have clutched it tightly . . .
What is there left except to tiptoe lightly
Out of the vault, and leave behind as lumber
Things now restored to their uneasy slumber . . .
And meekly linger . . . days of uncertain number?

—Rosemarie Schrödter

INTRODUCTION

NOTES
TO THE COMMENTARIES

MAIN EVENTS
IN THE LIFE OF
HENRY CORNELIUS AGRIPPA

NOTES TO THE COMMENTARIES

There are some esoteric teachings that, at the present time, are still being made available to the general reader in a very fragmentary form. Among these are the Talmud, works on the Kabbalah, works by Paracelsus, and works by Agrippa. Whereas there is no scarcity of anthologies of the "Hohenheimer" (Paracelsus, 1493–1541), his contemporary of Nettesheim (Agrippa, 1486–1535) has not found a sympathetic interpreter.[1]

This is probably because the main—though by no means the only—thrust of Paracelsus lies in the field of medicine, where we moderns feel more at ease; whereas Agrippa generally moves in the spheres of magic, divination, and numerology. On the one hand, we have the fiercely independent Paracelsus (*Alterius non sit qui sui esse potest,* Latin for: "If you can stand on your own two feet, don't lean on others!") who flung the standard medical textbooks of GALEN into St. John's fires, and wrote in a craggy but graphic German style, and devised his own terminology—a born empiric! On the other hand, we have Agrippa, a master of many foreign languages who possessed an encyclopedic knowledge of ancient authors, including literary stars of the least order of magnitude, who (as was usual in his day and age) were for the most part accepted uncritically by him. Out of all this he constructed a grandiose magical system, amalgamating in polished prose excerpts from the classics, the Bible, and the Kabbalah.

On making a cursory inspection of his opus, which is all we aim to do here, we become aware, with growing interest, that we can still accept much of what Agrippa says. By cutting out what is excessively abstruse—and all the great spirits of the Renaissance are abstruse at times—I have tried to uncover whatever can be supported by parallel cases. The present work is based on the German text originally published by J. SCHEIBLE (Stuttgart,

---

[1]   This book was compiled from Willy Schrödter's notes and published in German in 1967. In recent years Donald Tyson's annotated edition of the *Three Books of Occult Philosophy,* has been published by Llewellyn, St. Paul, MN, 1993, and brings this material to the English reader for the first time since Agrippa was published in English in the 17th century. Volume 1 had been reissued by Weiser in 1971, but the other two volumes were not published. In the meantime, these notes are still invaluable to students of Agrippa.

1856), which has been reprinted in other editions (Barsdorf, Berlin, 1916, and frequent reprints; Amonesta, Vienna, 1921).

The man who, when he was only 21 years old, founded a secret society in Paris for the study of paraphenomena, receiving at age 24 unstinted praise from the leading expert of the age (Trithemius); the man who gave the key to his Occult Philosophy in the following words:

Nos habitat, non tartara, sed nec sidera coeli,
Spiritus in nobis, qui viget, illa fecit[2]

is someone we really need to listen to and come to know, even today.

---

[2] "We are possessed neither by the infernal regions/nor by the stars of heaven/it is the spirit that rules in us/that performs these (marvels)." From a letter dated September 24, 1527 to the Augustinian monk Aurelius de Aquapendente (Ep. 14; L V.), one of his "oldest friends."

MAIN EVENTS
IN THE LIFE OF
HENRY CORNELIUS AGRIPPA

1486 Born in Cologne on September 14 into the wealthy von
Nettesheym family of knights. Read law at university and
received a comprehensive classical education. Learned
eight languages, fluent in six of them (Ep. 21; L. VII).

1507 Went to Paris where he founded and led a sodality or secret fraternity for practicing the occult sciences. Traveled
extensively in France, Italy, Germany, and England. (See
the letter written by the physician Landolf quoted at the
end of this curriculum vitae!)

1509 Delivered public lectures in Dôle (Burgundy) on "De verbo mirifico," a Kabbalisitic book by Johann REUCHLIN
(Capnio, 1455–1522). Became honorary lecturer at the university there, but fell foul of the clergy.

1510 Short trip to England on a secret mission. Then went to
stay in the monastery of St. Jakob in the suburb of
Würzburg with the "wizard-abbot" Johannes TRITHE-
MIUS (Heidenberg, 1462–1516). Reputedly, the latter gave
him arcane instruction and inspired him to compile the
celebrated *Three Books of Occult Philosophy* which, in the
same year, "became disseminated in garbled and corrupt
form throughout Germany, France, and Italy" (Author's
Preface). A mixed Platonic and Christian theosophy was
taught in this *De Occulta Philosophia*. It claimed that magic
was the art of gaining possession of the powers of the
higher world in order to rule the lower world. This loftiest
philosophy and most accomplished wisdom was natural

---

[1] The following books were used for data for this material: Kurt Aram, *Magie und Mystik*
[Magic and Mysticism], Berlin, 1929, 263–271; Carl Kiesewetter, *Geschichte des neueren
Occultismus* [A History of Modern Occultism] !st ed., Leipzig, 1891, 1–39; H. Morley,
Life of Cornelius Agrippa, London, 1856 (2 vols.); J. Orsier, *Henri Cornélis Agrippa, sa vie et
son œuvre d'après sa correspondance* [The Life and Work of Henry Cornelius Agrippa
Based on his Correspondence], Paris, 1911; and H. Prost, *Corneille Agrippa*, Paris, 1881–
1882 (2 vols.).

magic when ruling earth things, celestial magic when invoking the stars, and ceremonial magic when commanding spirits and demons.

1511   Imperial counselor; superintendent of mines.

1512   Captain in the army of the Emperor MAXIMILIAN I (1493–1519) fighting the Venetians. Knighted in the field for bravery. Obtained an LL.D. and M.D. (Ep. 21; L. VII).

1513   Pope LEO X (1513–1521) commended him in a letter of July 12 for his zeal for the papacy.

1515   Lecture on Hermes Trismegistus in Pavia.

1518   Advocate in Metz. Came into conflict with the Inquisition by defending alleged "witches."

1519   Consequent return to Cologne.

1521   Death of his first wife. Moved to Geneva and practiced medicine.

1523   Physician in Fribourg (Switzerland). Remarried.

1524   Physician in Lyon. Court physician to LOUISE of Savoy (1476–1531), the mother of FRANCIS I (1515–1547). Fell out of favor because he would not cast a political horoscope (Ep. 37; L. IV).

1528   Gained the reputation of miracle doctor in Antwerp. His second wife died in an epidemic.

1529   Archivist and historiographer to the Regent MARGARET of Austria (1507–1530), Stadholder of the Netherlands. Soon in fresh conflict with the clergy.

1530   His *De Occulta Philosophia* published in Antwerp. Briefly imprisoned in Brussels.

1532   Visited the Archbishop of Trier, Count Hermann of WIED, to whom he had dedicated his *De Occulta Philosophia.*

1533   An enlarged and improved edition brought out in Cologne. Then he went to Bonn, where Johannes WEYER [Wierus] of Gravelines came to study medicine under him.

1535   Divorced his third wife (whom he had married in Mechlin). Moved to Grenoble, where he died on February 18 in the house of a prominent citizen and was buried by the Dominicans.

LANDOLFUS, a physician, wrote to AGRIPPA from Lyon among other things: "The man who delivers my letter . . . is an eager enquirer into esoteric matters (*rerum arcanarum curiosus indagator*) and a free man (*homo liber*). I should be grateful if you would find out what you can about the man, and I hope he will inform you of the goal of his endeavors. For in my opinion he is not far from the goal (a scopo). . . . Therefore speed from north to south, equipped with the wings of Mercury. Pick up—I beg you—the scepter of highest authority (*Jovis sceptra*) and receive this person into our company if he wishes to take the vows laid down in our statutes (*si in nostra velit jurare capitula, nostro sodalicio adscitum face*). Our other companions (*ceteri commilitones nostri*) await your arrival. So trim your sails joyfully and hasten to the harbor (*portum*) of our mutual happiness!"[2]

---

[2] From: Hartlaub, GuStav Friedrich: *Giorgiones Geheimnis* [Giorgione's Secret], Munich 1925; 19. Hartlaub quotes from Ludwig Keller's *Vorgeschichte der Freimaurerei* [Antecedents of Freemasonry], published by the Comenius-Gesellschaft in Berlin.

Henricus Cornelius Agrippa
Doctor of Law and Doctor of Medicine

FIRST BOOK

ON NATURAL MAGIC

Natural magic is what I call a certain hidden knowledge of the secrets of nature, by which, when one has recognized the nature, properties, concealed powers, sympathies, and antipathies of individual things, one can produce certain effects which appear strange or even miraculous to those who are uninformed of their causes.

—Caspar SCHOTT S.J. (1608–1666)
Magia universalis naturae et artis, 1657

As soon as the common people see something out of the ordinary, they ignorantly imagine that demons are responsible for it, and they look on any product of natural or mathematical philosophy as a miracle.

—Henry Cornelius Agrippa
(Book II; Ch. 1)

Since there is a natural connection between everything in the universe and the whole of it is a manifold of powers, which attract and repel one another in various ways and by means of sympathy (elective affinity) are forcibly united in one life, it follows that a natural magic, theurgy, and divination must exist.

—PLOTINUS (205-270)

THE AKASHIC RECORDS
(Chapter 6)

*And now all that remains for me to do is to speak of Air
. . . (In the same way), like a divine mirror, it collects
the forms of all natural or artificial objects as well as
the sound of every spoken word, retains them, takes
them with it, and on entering the bodies of humans or
animals through their pores, it impresses the images of
these things on them, not only when they are asleep
but also when they are awake, and so gives rise to various wonderful dreams, premonitions, and prophecies.*

The technical term *Akashic Records* was coined by the founder of
Anthroposophy, Dr. Rudolf STEINER (1861–1925). The Indian
word *Akasha* means "space"[1] as well as what fills it—the Ether.
Agrippa treats Air as a vehicle, and heads his chapter: "Concerning the wonderful nature of Water, Air, and Winds." The abbé
Alphonse Louis CONSTANT (1810–1875), who as a Kabbalist
called himself ELIPHAS LEVI ZOHED, used the term "Astral
light" for the same concept. "The underlying idea here is that
every occurrence impresses itself on the Ether, and every
thought vibrates in it for all eternity. Because thoughts are a form
of energy, like light, though a finer, or 'astral' (Latin for 'starry')
light, then according to what Dr. Julius Robert von MAYER
(1814–1878) called in 1842 'the law of the conservation of energy'
they can never be lost."[2]

The Kabbalah is familiar with the "supreme book,"[3] Is-
lam with the "eternal book,"[4] and the Rosicrucians with the *Liber
Mundi*[5] in which all the thoughts, words, and actions of individuals and of humanity as a whole are inscribed forever. Prolonged
"imbibing from the spheres" (GOETHE) through the appropriate "tuning in" by those who are trained or naturally gifted
along these lines, draws the "etheric matrix" down here from

---

[1] Dr. Guido Huber, *Akaça—der mystische Raum* [Akasha—Mystic Space], Zurich, 1955.
[2] Willy Schrödter, "Schöpfer oder Antenne?" [Creator or Antenna?] in *Natur & Kultur,*
Folge I. Munich–Solln, 1959, 16f.
[3] Esarah Maimeroth in Zohar (fol. 49).
[4] Koran, Sura X, ajât 62; Sura VI, ajât 59.
[5] *Fama Fraternitatis RC,* Cassel, 1614.

this "sea of glass" and "galvanizes" them into new life. Clair-voyant visions of past events, discoveries of all sorts, and poetic inspiration originate here. The poet is more or less a "creative genius" or an "antenna."[6] At this point, our author has anticipat-ed the theory of "etheric primitive forms" advocated by people like EICHORN.[7, 8, 9]

HAUNTED PLACES
(Chapter 6)

This explains why many people are seized with sudden fear or have a sense of oppression on passing a spot where a person has been killed, or where a recently bur-ied body lies. The atmosphere of such a place is full of frightful images of the murder, and these images un-settle the spirit of the individual who breathes it in, and beget fear and anxiety. Everything that makes a sudden strong impression disturbs nature.

It was the Ariosoph, Guido von LIST (1848–1919) who first ex-pressed the belief that an act of violence impregnates the place where it is done; and the dowser Anton KELLER (1881–1946) ac-tually photographed such places and obtained images of the at-tacker or the victim.[10]

Usually hauntings occur in localities where crimes have been committed. With this in mind, the independent Viennese researcher Emanuel CIHLAR (born 1888) used to spend the

---

[6] Willy Schrödter, *Abenteuer mit Gedanken* [Adventures with Ideas], Freiburg/B., 1954, 29f; "Der Dichter—ein Seher" [The Poet—A Seer] in *Neue Wissenschaft*, No. 4, Oberengstringen/Zürich, 168 f.

[7] Dr. Gust. Eichhorn, *Vererbung, Gedächtnis und transzendentale Erinnerung* [Heredity, Memory, and Transcendental Recollection], Stuttgart, 1909.

[8] Dr. Ferdinand Maack, *Elias Artista*, Berlin, 1913.

[9] Wilh. Gädicke, *Das siderische Pendel, die Wünschelrute und andere siderische Detektoren, Strahlenindikatoren und Odoskope* [The Pendulum, Divining Rod, and other Sidereal Detectors, Radiation Indicators and Odoscopes], Bad Oldesloe, 1924, 25 f.

[10] Willy Schrödter, *Grenzwissenschaftliche Versuche für jedermann* [Paranormal Research for All], Freiburg 1959.

night in such localities and saw revealing images in his dreams (incubation).

Carl HUTER (1861–1912) has established that even "dead" matter, such as stone and metal, possesses "sensitivity," or the capacity for storing impressions and releasing them later. Stones can speak. They have a dim awareness and retain what they have "experienced." This explains the sinister nature of many sites and the sanctity of others, both of which are readily perceived by sensitives.[11] I have given the name "Mana places"[12] to these sites. What is more, we say that certain houses have a "psychic infection."[13] Gustav MEYRINK (1868–1932) says of his character Christopher Taubenschlag: Being open to the occult, he felt "as if the magnetic atmosphere of the place preserved what happened and then released it from time to time."[14]

TELEPATHY
(Chapter 6)

Quite naturally, and without any superstition or intervention of spirits, it is possible for one person to transmit his thoughts to another over any (even unknown) distance however far, within a very short time. Even if the time taken cannot be measured exactly, in no case are more than twenty-four hours required. I understand the art of doing this and have often tried it out. The abbot Trithemius, too, understands it and practiced it at one time.[15]

---

[11] Werner Altpeter, *Zeichen der Zeit: Kritik am modernen Menschen* [Signs of the Times: A Critique of Modern Humanity], Frankfurt/Main, 1956, 39.

[12] Willy Schrödter, "Mana-Orte" [Mana places] in "Meistergedanken" [Master Thoughts] in *Natur & Kultur,* Series1-2, January–June, Munich–Solln, 1962, 64.

[13] Willy Schrödter, Physisch [sic] verseuchte Wohnungen [Physically Infected Dwellings: the *Physisch* = "physically" must be a misprint of *Psychisch* = "psychically" found in the main text. Tr.] in "Allerlei okkulte Merkwürdigkeiten" [A Miscellany of Occult Marvels] in *Die Andere Welt,* vol. 9, September, Freiburg, 1963, 693 f.

[14] Gustav Meyrink, *Der Weiße Dominikaner* [The White Dominican], Vienna, 1921, 232.

[15] Kiesewetter says, "I may mention as a parallel that, according to the London S.P.R., telepathic phenomena occur not later than 12 hours after the death of the transmitter."

Seeing that Agrippa's title for this chapter is, in part, "Of the Wonderful Nature of . . . Air, and Winds," it is worth mentioning at the outset that the Tibetans call their telepathic news agency, "messages through the air," or "messages on the winds."[16] As I have already dealt with this subject in considerable detail elsewhere, the reader is referred to some of my other books and articles.[17]

Johannes TRITHEMIUS (1462–1516), properly Heidenberg, of Trittenheim on the Mosel, ended up as abbot of the monastery of St. Jakob in the suburbs of Würzburg, and was one of the leading paranormal investigators of his age. Having stayed with him for a "long time," Agrippa submitted *Occult Philosophy* to him for his opinion, and had received his full endorsement on April 8, 1510. His amenuensis, Johannes WIER (or Wierus, or Weier, 1513–1585), reports in his *De magis* (C. V; P. III):

"Because AGRIPPA did not leave his lodgings for weeks at a time and yet knew all that was going on in various countries, scandalmongers put it about that his dog (a black one called 'Monsieur') was a devil who kept him informed of everything."[18]

Possibly Agrippa was linked telepathically all over the world with adepts at his own stage of development. A fairly recent example of a "brain-radio news service" of this kind is that of the Spaniard, Count Juan PARAVICINO Y ARTEAGA, who "laid aside his old garment" at an advanced age in Toledo in 1952. The papers he left behind, letters that arrived posthumously from Brazil, China, India, Mongolia, Persia, Peru, and the USA supply the evidence. What is more, the adept used to place himself in a deep trance for weeks at a time, presumably to send his soul traveling.

In 1937–1938, during the search carried out by the Australian polar aviator Sir Hubert George WILKINS (1888–1958) for the

---

[16] Alexandra David–Neel, *Magic and Mystery in Tibet,* Dover, New York, 1971.

[17] Willy Schrödter, *A Rosicrucian Notebook,* Samuel Weiser, York Beach, ME, 1992; *Offenbarungen eines Magiers* [The Revelations of a Magician], Warpke-Billerbeck, 1955; 12, 70; *History of Energy Transference,* Samuel Weiser, York Beach, ME, 1999; "Telepathischer Nachrichtendienst" ["Telepathic News Agency"] in *Das Neue Licht* (No. 12), 1951, 228 f, No. 1, 1959, 22 f; "Telepathischer Nachrichtendienst" in *Neue Wissenschaft* (No. 11–12). Oberengstringen/Zürich, 1956, 336 f.

[18] Kurt Aram, (Hans Fischer) *Magie und Mystik* [Magic and Mysticism], Berlin, 1929, 270–271.

missing Russian polar aviator S. LEWANEWSKY, the American writer Harold SHERMAN, who was a friend of the former, remained in verified constant telepathic communication with him. "From November 1937 to March 1938 sixty-eight highly successful cases of telepathic communication were achieved in this way."[19] When the first American nuclear submarine Nautilus commanded by Captain ANDERSON made her sensational undersea voyage between July 25 and August 10, 1959, mainly beneath the Arctic ice, telepathic contact with the mainland was kept up. The telepath in the submarine was naval lieutenant JONES, and the telepath on the mainland was student SMITH of Duke University, Durham (North Carolina) under the supervision of Colonel William BOWERS at the Westinghouse Center for Special Research in Friendship (Maryland). Five "Morse signals" had been prearranged (star, cross, circle, square, three wavy lines) and the success rate was 70 percent. The tests on this type of communication were run because radio telegraphy was impossible under pack-ice![20] Finally, mention should also be made of the so-called "coconut radio" on Tahiti.[21] The so-called "primitives are miles ahead of us in this respect!"[22]

CONCAVE MIRROR / CAMERA OBSCURA / SOLAR MICROSCOPE
(Chapter 6)

There are certain mirrors by means of which one can project on the air, even quite a long way from these mirrors, any given images which are regarded by inexperienced people as specters or ghosts of the departed, whereas they are nothing more than empty mirror

---

[19] Dr. Peter Ringger, *Parapsychologie* [Parapsychology], Zürich, 1957, 34 f; Wilkins and Sherman, *Thoughts Through Space,* C. & R. Anthony, Inc., New York 1951.
[20] Louis Pauwels and Jacques Bergier, *The Morning of the Magicians,* Stein & Day, New York, 1977; Avon, 1980.
[21] Max Freedom Long, *Secret Science Behind Miracles,* De Vorss, Marina del Rey, CA, 1948.
[22] Ernesto Bozzano, *Übersinnliche Erscheinungen bei Naturvölkern* [Supernatural Phenomena Involving Primitive Races], Sammlung Dalp, vol. 52, Bern, 1948, 30 f.

*Johannes Trithemius
(Real name Heidenberg; 1462-1516) of
Trittenheim bei Trier. Abbot since 1483, first in
Sponheim bei Kreuznach, then in the monastery of
St. Jakob at Würzburg-Vorstadt.*

images devoid of all life and produced by human agency. It is also a known fact that, in a completely dark place into which a ray of sunlight can be admitted through a very small aperture, a piece of white paper or a plain mirror placed in the path of that ray of light will display everything that is happening outside in the sunshine.

We know that Abbot TRITHEMIUS caused "ghosts of the departed" to appear,[23] apparently (believe it or not) by a magic lantern such as had been used even earlier for this purpose by Taoist magicians. "Thus one such illusionist won the favor of the Emperor Han Wu-ti (140–87) by causing the strikingly life-like picture of his dead mistress to be projected by a magic lantern from behind a screen."[24] And when Trithemius showed the Emperor Maximilian I (1493–1519), the "last of the knights," an "illusory counterfeit" of his deceased consort Maria of Burgundy, the Emperor said sternly, "Monk, have done with this foolery!"[25]

The *camera obscura* (Latin: dark chamber) or pin-hole camera was invented in 1321 by Levi ben GERSON. Brockhaus defines it as a "device by which the light entering a dark room through a very small hole throws an (inverted) image of external objects on the opposite wall." And adds that it was "improved by placing a convex lens in the aperture, and changing the chamber into a dark box with a ground glass rear wall for viewing or making traces of images while one is looking at the box from the outside (the *camera clara*). The photographic camera, like the human eye, is a *camera obscura*."

According to the latest research, the Jewish philosopher, mathematician, astronomer, and Bible commentator, Rabbi Levi ben Gerson (Gersonides, 1288–1344) was not the original inventor of the camera obscura, seeing that the Arab mathematician and natural philosopher Ibn al–Haitham (Latin: Alhazan, 965–1038) had already experimented with it (Dr. Sigrid Hunke). "It

---

[23] Carl Kiesewetter, *Faust in der Geschichte und Tradition* [Faust in History and Tradition], Berlin, 1921.

[24] Ed. Erkes, *Chinesische Literatur* [Chinese Literature], Breslau, 1922, 60.

[25] As footnote 23 above. German readers may be able to find a diagram called "Optics I" in the Brockhaus, *Handbuch des Wissens* [Handbook of Knowledge] showing how an "upright real image of a bunch of flowers held upside down is produced in the air by a concave mirror."

was invented by the later Greeks, the Arabs only copied it" (Dr. Walter Koch).

A "solar microscope" (*microscope solaire*) is (according to Larousse) "a simple projector consisting of a lens that throws on a screen a real[26] magnified image of any object strongly illuminated by the sun."

PROJECTIONS ON THE MOON
(Chapter 6)

An even more wonderful phenomenon is when on a clear night painted pictures or written letters are exposed in a certain way to the rays of the full moon, whereupon the forms of such pictures and letters reproduce themselves in the air, are drawn upward, and then reflected with the moon's rays in such a way that another person who knows what is being done can read and recognize them immediately in the disk of the moon. This art, which I regard as very useful for besieged castles and towns wishing to send secret messages, was formerly used by Pythagoras and today is known to only a few apart from myself.

I should not like to dismiss out of hand the personal experience alleged by the "demonic knight" (Aram's name for him) when, in our own day, the techno-wizard Nicola TESLA (1856–1943) once declared that "it might be possible at new moon for him to produce on the dark disk of the moon a stupendous luminous spot that would be visible from Earth with the naked eye."[27]

---

[26] "Real" as opposed to "virtual" is a technical term in optics. Light rays "really" pass through a "real" image. Tr. note.

[27] Lambert Binder, "Porträt eines Technomagiers" [Portrait of a Techno-Wizard] in *Mensch & Schicksal,* No. 21, January 15, Villach 1953, 5; Willy Schrödter, *Grenzwiss. Versuche* [Parapsychological Research for All] chapter on "The Moon," 149 f. [TESLA was probably looking ahead to something like our modern laser. What AGRIPPA meant is better described by LA MOTTE FOUQUÉ in *Head Master Rhenfried and his Family:* "... a magical mirror that ... shall retain the moon's beams in such a manner as to exhibit by secret reflection on the surface everything that passes upon Earth's sphere in succession, according as such magic mirror shall be directed and applied." *The German Novelists,* translated and edited by Thomas Roscoe, London ca. 1827, p. 321. Tr. note.

What is more, Dr. Kenzaburo TOYODA of the Japanese University Meiji has stated that, when studying the moon through a telescope during a night in September 1958, he made out the words PYAX and JWA under the Sea of Serenity to the left of the Sea of Tranquility. "The letters were black and perfectly legible. Two other witnesses also saw the letters," according to "Mainichi" one of Japan's leading papers.[28] It is obvious that the imperial army captain, who was knighted in the field for bravery (Ep. 21. L. VII), would employ this art for military purposes. PYTHAGORAS (580-493), the mystical philosopher and mathematician of Samos, who taught astral travel, eternal recurrence, the harmony of the spheres, eurhythmy, numerology, and monotheism, discovered the fundamental geometric theorem named for him, founded in Southern Italy the Pythagorean social-reforming and religious secret society, and left behind for posterity his *Golden Verses*.

PERPETUAL LAMPS
(Chapter 9)

Finally, there are inextinguishable fire, incombustible oils, and perpetual lamps, which cannot be doused by wind, water, or anything else; something quite incredible except for a world-famous lamp of the same sort that once shone in the temple of Venus. A piece of asbestos burned inside it which never went out after being thoroughly ignited.

Such perpetual lamps were also a speciality of the Rosicrucian Order. When the tomb of the Order's reorganizer, A. Christian ROSENCREUTZ (Rosicrucius, 1378–1484) was opened "this vault was well lit; although it was never illuminated by the sun but, just as brightly, by an artificial sun suspended from the ceiling."[29]

In 1534 there was found in the grave of Tullia (died 45 B.C.), the daughter of Marcus Tullius CICERO (106–43 B.C.) a lamp of this kind, which was extinguished by a current of air. Two such lamps

---

[28] "UFO-Bulletin," Sydney (Australia), July, 1959.
[29] *Fama Fraternitatis R C,* Cassel, 1614.

were hidden at the time of the dissolution of the monasteries in England (ca. 1533–1539) during the reign of Henry VIII (1491–1547). They had been burning since the 14th century, and are now preserved in Leyden museum in The Netherlands.[30] In Vatopedi monastery on Mt. Athos, even today the pendant silver lamp on the right of the ikon of the Blessed Virgin burns with an inextinguishable flame, as it has been burning for centuries. "It has not been replenished with oil, and yet . . ."[31] We ought not to be so ready to say "impossible"; the French inventor of gas lighting, the engineer and chemist Philippe LEBON (1769–1804), who patented his *thermo-lampes* in 1799, must have had it cross his mind that a lamp with no wick simply could not burn, because it would break the laws of nature!

Nature has presented us with the oldest "perpetual lamp" in the form of a gas flame that was mentioned by Homer and throws out three-foot-high columns of fire from the summit of the Yarnatsch (Asia Minor).

FIREPROOF WOOD
(Chapter 9)

On the other hand, wood or indeed any inflammable material can be specially treated to prevent it being damaged by fire.

In the Black Forest today, one still occasionally comes across a lonely farmstead with an open hearth from which, for hundreds of years, flames have leaped to the ceiling beam without catching the house on fire. To make timber fireproof, it must be cut at a certain asterism of the moon and then prepared. Renaissance "Books of Knowledge" are full of the relevant formulas. A more modern one ends its recipe with the words: "This discovery is very old: TOBELIUS in Book Two of his *Pantagruel* (in chapter 50), mentions a wooden tower which Sylla was unable to set alight because Archilaus, governor of the city of Pyrus in Attica, had completely coated it with alum in the reign of King Mithridates."[32]

---

[30] Schrödter, *A Rosicrucian Notebook* (chapter on perpetual lamps); Thornton Wilder, *Die Cabala* [The Kabbalah], Fischer-Bücherei No. 189, Frankfurt, 1957, 128.
[31] Dr. Franz Spunda, *Der hl. Berg Athos* [The Holy Mountain, Athos], Leipzig, 1928, 169.
[32] Dr. Wilhelm Rinne, *Das goldene Büchlein der Wunder od. nützliches Allerlei etc.* [The Little Golden Book of Wonders, or a Useful Miscellany, etc.], Heilbronn, 1843, 45, No. 82.

An English POW, several hundred years ago, "discovered a mixture that prevented timber coated with it from being burned."[33] But perhaps it is not even necessary for the wood to be treated in order to become fireproof. Listen to what the painter Lucian REICH (1817–1900) had to say on the subject more than a hundred years ago:

> *Standing in the Schwarzenbachtal near Neustadt (Black Forest) are several large isolated farms, sometimes called "the heathen farms." Old-timers say that heathen built them and that the structures were fireproof, although made entirely of wood. I should like to make it clear that I set no store by superstitions, but what I have seen with my own eyes leads me to conclude that if the beams above the hearth had been made of ordinary wood they would have gone up in flames long ago, due to the blazing fires lit underneath. The heathen, according to our ancestors, knew the secret of cutting the timber when the moon and planets were in the right signs of the Zodiac. Therefore it was not easily set alight; nor did it lose its usefulness through shrinkage or warping.*[34]

In any case, it is a known fact that no Brazilian or Argentinean timber merchant will have wood chopped when the moon is waning, as otherwise the wood splinters.[35] The same rule is observed in Scotland.[36] One of the last perfectly preserved covered wooden bridges in Germany crosses the Donau in Beuron (Wttbg.). The method of preserving the timber, employed by the monks nearly 300 years ago, has not been handed down.

---

32 con't.

Lucius Cornelius Sylla (Sulla; 136–78 B.C.) was a Roman dictator who conquered the King of Pontus, Mithridates VII, the Great (123–63). The wars waged on Rome by this monarch lasted almost without a break from 90 through 63 B.C.

[33] Dr. Wilhelm Rinne, p. 49 f., No. 92.

[34] Lucian Reich, *Wanderblüten a.d. Gedenkbuch eines Malers* [Wayside Blossoms from a Painter's Logbook], Karlsruhe, 1855, 104.

[35] Carl Kiesewetter, *Die Geheimwissenschaften* [The Occult Sciences], Leipzig, 1895, 246 footnote 2.

[36] Rinne, 16–17, No. 34. Willy Schrödter, "Vom Einfluß des Mondes auf Erdendinge" [The Influence of the Moon on Terrestrial Things] in *Okkulte Stimme*, No. 30, July, Brunswick, 1953, 11.

HANDLING RED-HOT IRON UNHARMED
(Chapter 9)

If a certain ointment is smeared over the hands, one can hold glowing iron, or thrust the hand into molten metal, or walk bodily into the fire, without suffering any harm, and can perform other similar feats.

I wrote about the following incident in my book:

> *In the memoirs of the stage illusionist Jasper MASKE-LYNE, which were published in 1938, we read in connection with World War I that the British Admiralty had ascertained in various naval battles that a time came when the gunners had to stop firing because the ordnance had become so hot. Now one of the officers at the Admiralty remembered that MASKELYNE had picked up red-hot iron with his hands during a variety theater performance. It could therefore be inferred that he knew of some means of protection from heat. Contact was made with him and, as it turned out, he possessed a secret of this sort that he had brought from India. A paste was quickly prepared and the hands of the naval gunners were smeared with it. During the engagements they were then able to handle the guns much more often and for longer periods, even when the equipment was almost red hot.[37]*

"Fire-walking" in India and Japan, and on the islands of Hawaii, Harvey, Sunda, Fiji, Trinidad, and Mauritius, the "fire dance" of the Bulgarian "Nestinari" and the immunity to this element of the Turkish Dervishes, is not a chemical, but a psychological, matter. By song or instrumental music, the participants separate their spirits from their bodies ("Statuvolence") and do not feel pain when in this trance state, or suffer from burns.[38]

---

[37] Willy Schrödter, *Pflanzen-Geheimnisse* [Plant Secrets], Warpke-Billerbeck, 1957, 100–101.

[38] Ernesto Bozzano, *Übersinnliche Erscheinungen bei Naturvölkern* [Supernatural Phenomena in Primitive Races], chapter on "Die Feuerprobe" [The Ordeal by Fire], Sammlung Dalp, No. 52, Bern, 1948, 192 f; Guido Huber, *Übersinnliche Gaben* [Supernatural Talents], chapter 2, "Die Feuerfestigkeit" [Imperviousness to Fire], Zürich, 1959. Prof. G.A. van Rijnberk, *Les Métasciences biologiques* [The Biological Metasciences], chapter

It is up to the reader to decide whether or not the "Song of the Three Holy Children" who were able to emerge from the fiery furnace unscathed, points to a phenomenon produced by ecstasy.[39] Our author attached special importance to this song (I: 96; III: 186).

The immunity from fire of the Scottish medium Daniel Douglas HOME (1833–1886) was witnessed by the famous English chemist and physicist Sir William CROOKES (1832–1919).[40] In the Middle Ages there was an ordeal by fire in which molten lead was poured over the hands of a person accused of some crime; if no harm came to him, he was acquitted. Back in 1962, the radio program presenter and physicist Arthur GARRAT, his wife PALOMA, and the journalist Noel WITHCOMB, underwent this ordeal in Battersea, South London, after immersing their hands in a solvent and then in ammonia. This procedure protected them from burns and their hands were only blackened. KEYSTONE photographed the event!

---

38 con't.

on "Résistance au feu" [Resistance to Fire], Paris: Adyar, 1952, 164–165; Dr. Karl Schmidt, *Die okkulten Wissenschaften im Lichte der Wissenschaft (Grundzüge einer Magiologie)* [The Occult Sciences in the Light of Science: Outlines of a Theory of Magic], chapter on "Feuerlaufen" [Fire-Walking], Sammlung Göschen No. 872, Berlin & Leipzig, 1923, 100 f; Dr. Carl Vett, *Seltsame Erlebnisse in einem Derwischkloster* [Strange Experiences in a Dervish Monastery], Straßburg, 1931, 243 f; Dr. Peter Panoff, "Tanz auf glühenden Kohlen" [Dance on Red-Hot Coals] in *Okkulte Stimme,* Part 2, February, 1957, 20 f; Anonymous, "Ich schritt über rotglühenden Steine" [I Walked Across Red-Hot Stones] in *Die andere Welt,* Part 2, February, 1957, 5 f; Max Freedom Long, *The Secret Science Behind Miracles,* chapter on fire walking, De Vorss Marina del Rey, CA, 1948; Carl du Prel, *Studien aus dem Gebiete der Geheimwissenschaften* [Studies from the Field of the Occult Sciences], chapter on "Das Phänomen der Feuerfestigkeit" [The Phenomenon of Immunity to Fire], Leipzig, 1905; Wilhelm Moufang, *Magier, Mächte und Mysterien* [Magicians, Powers, and Mysteries], Heidelberg, 1954, 258, 344 f.

[39] Daniel, ch. 3, "The prayer of Azarias" (supplement to Daniel 3); "The Song of the Three Holy Children" (continuation of supplement). [These passages belong to the Apocrypha. Tr.]

[40] Dr. Karl Schmidt, *Die Okkolten Wissenschaften. . . .,* 100 f. D. D. Home, *Lights and Shadows of Spiritualism,* London, 1883.

THE SUCKING FISH
(Chapter X and Chapter XX)

A small fish, called the sucking fish, tames the fury of the winds and the stormy sea so that, even if the tempest rages and the wind fills all their sails, this little fish is able to stop ships simply by contact and prevent them from making further progress.

In the section on the compatibility of certain plants and animals we mention that this fish lives in "epizoic partnership" with the shark. We would simply add that the sucking fish (*Echeneis*) is a poor swimmer, and therefore attaches itself to other marine animals (sharks, turtles) by means of a sucker on the top of its head and on the forepart of its back. It also takes hold of ships and lets itself be carried along by them. In Northern Australia, Zanzibar, Cuba, and other places with tropical or temperate waters, anglers make use the sucking propensity of the up-to-three-feet-long sucking fish (*Echeneis naucrates L.*) by dangling it from their lines when fishing for turtles. Once again we find that there is some truth in many an old tale![41]

In any case, as far as the sucking fish is concerned, Agrippa is only repeating what was said about it in Renaissance and Ancient times. He also makes clear in chapter XXI that he is merely playing the part of a reporter.

ALCHEMY
(Chapter XIV)

Agrippa has no particular reputation as an alchemist; although, admittedly, he did make friends with someone in Antwerp in 1528 by flashing some rather wild alchemical promises. However it was in keeping with his nature to take an interest in this contemporary problem. His alchemical theory took the doctrine of Pythagoras as its cosmogenetic starting point:

---

[41] Willy Schrödter, *Tier-Geheimnisse* [Animal Secrets], Warpke-Billerbeck, 1960, 230.

Now since the soul, the Primum mobile, is autonomous and self-activated, but the body, or matter, is strictly speaking motionless and is set apart from the soul, therefore the old philosophers say that something intermediate is required that, as it were, is not a body, but a soul, and on the other hand, is not a soul but a body— something that binds the soul and body together. Just such a medium is the World Spirit, known to us as the Quintessence (fifth essence), for it does not consist of the four elements, but is a fifth above and beyond them.

The Hermetic axiom "As above so below" (Latin: *inferior quod superior*)[42] comes to mind here; also the "microcosmic human" is tripartite (Greek: *Trichotomê*):

This spirit is in exactly the same form in the World Body as our spirit is in the human body; for just as the powers of our soul communicate themselves to our members through the spirit, so the power of the World Soul flows through everything by means of the Quintessence. There is nothing in the whole world that does not have some spark of its power; however it flows most strongly into the objects that possess most of this spirit. It is obtained from the light of the stars to the extent that the said objects are capable of receiving their radiations. . . . However, this spirit can be even more useful to us when we know how to separate it as much as possible from the other elements, or at least how to employ such things, on the whole, that possess the said spirit in abundance. Things in which this spirit is less absorbed in the body and less bound to matter, operate more powerfully and fully, and produce more quickly what resembles them, because all generative and seminal powers are contained in it.

---

[42] The law of the correspondence of the little world (microcosm) of the human being to the great world (macrocosm) of God, spirits, and the stars, which was so important to the Renaissance philosophers, has never been more clearly expressed than in the *Timæus* of PLATO (Aristokles: 427–347 B.C.). See also *Paracelsus, Neuplatonismus und indische Geheimlehre* [Paracelsus, Neoplatonism and Indian Secret Doctrine], St. Gallen, 1947, 9–10) by the late Swiss Paracelsian researcher, Dr. J. STREBEL.

Now Agrippa comes to actual practice:

For which reason the alchemists try to separate this spirit from silver and gold; and if it is properly separated and extracted, and then combined with a metal of any sort, silver or gold will be produced immediately. Now we understand this secret and have already seen it put into practice; but we could not make more gold than the weight of the gold from which we had extracted the spirit. For as that spirit is the outer form and not an inner one, it cannot transmute an imperfect body into a perfect one beyond its own limits. Nevertheless, I will not deny that such a thing can happen in another way.

From which it would appear that Agrippa had seen how someone extracted its quintessence from the metal kingdom, the "spirit of silver," or the "spirit of gold" as the case might be, removing the essence of silver or gold and "coloring" a base metal with it. But "projection" on the latter could not yield more than the original mass of noble metal. The more normal "multiplication" did not occur. Agrippa realized that the process was not ideal, and did not deny that "an imperfect body can be transmuted into a perfect one in another way." The "Sons and Daughters of Art" will refer back to the sentence: "The World Spirit is obtained from the light of the stars to the extent that the said objects are capable of receiving their radiations." And in the words "in another way" they will discern "another kingdom" more suited than metals to the storage of "stellar radiation." One naturally thinks of the dissimilar, living vegetable kingdom; and also of the so-called "star jelly" (French: *crachat de lune*), a strange alga known as *nostoc,* which in former days was thought to have a sidereal origin.[43]

We can only wonder at the intuition of the old chemists, because according to recent research algae accumulate radium very readily.[44] Now additives containing radium may well have

---

[43] Willy Schrödter, *Pflanzen-Geheimnisse* [Plant Secrets], 77 f.
[44] "Radium aus Algen" [Radium from Algae] in *Koralle,* vol. 14, April 6, 1941, Berlin 365; Willy Schrödter, *Streifzug ins Ungewohnte* [A Trip into the Unusual], Freiburg/Brsg., 1949.

been essential ingredients in some notoriously effective tinctures.[45] Paracelsus (1493–1541) hunted for algae of a certain type in the High Tauern (Prof. HABERLANDT).

It is a well-known fact that gold can be made artificially and quite quickly nowadays in large and expensive pieces of apparatus. The question is this: could the alchemists have done the same with the simplest of apparatus but over the period of a year or more? There is incontestable historical evidence that they did so.[46] Finally, each plant is an alchemist;[47] so is our digestive system which "transmutes" chyme into flesh and bone, nerves and brain, and so is the fruit-grower who improves the wild crab-apple to obtain a Calville apple.[48]

ORGANOTHERAPY
(Chapter XV)

It is a recognized fact among physicians that the brain brings healing to the brain and the lungs bring healing to the lungs.

Indeed, it was a recognized fact long before the days of Agrippa: the ancient Chinese used pig's lungs for pulmonary disease.[49] Organotherapists of the female sex were the hags or witches, who can be traced back to antiquity. To some extent they used parts of human organs; and when they bought or stole children and slaughtered them, this was not as a sacrifice to their masters but to obtain organ extracts, as even in our own times the black cobbler Jeremiah of Trinidad intended to obtain, from the head of a fat boy, the "oil of Vishnu" which was said to restore virility.[50] This belief had made its way from North India to that little

---

[45] Dr. Erich Bischoff, *Der Sieg der Alchemie* [The Victory of Alchemy], Berlin, 1925, 131.
[46] Dr. Karl Christoph Schmieder, *Geschichte der Alchemie* [A History of Alchemy], new impression, Ulm/Donau, 1959.
[47] Willy Schrödter, *Pflanzen-Geheimnisse* [Plant Secrets], 66 f.
[48] P. R. Eichelter, *Vom Goldmachen* [Gold-Making], Hattenheim/Rhg, 1924, 8.
[49] Adolf Reitz, *Die Schöpferkräfte der Chemie* [The Creative Powers of Chemistry], Stuttgart, 1939, 185.
[50] Alma M. Karlin, *Der Todesdorn* [The Death-Thorn], Berlin, 1933, 290.

island of the Lesser Antilles at the mouth of the Orinoco; the sorcerers who employ this horrible practice are called "Moniai." I see in this word the Latin *Mumia,* which was used in the Renaissance for the "Od-carriers" which were prepared from excretions (sweat, urine, feces, spittle; also blood), plus organ parts (hair, fingernails, etc.), plus if necessary, soiled underwear belonging to the subject. The executioner was often approached by those who were looking for human organs. Formerly the parts were eaten just as they were; today, when taken orally, it is in the form of medicaments (*Haematogen:* from cows' blood for anemia; *Oophonin:* from cows' or pigs' ovaries for diseases of the uterus; *Cerebrin:* from calves' brains for nervous disorders, etc.). In the overwhelming majority of cases nowadays, animal organic extracts are injected (e.g., *Cor-Hormon* from embryonic animal hearts for neurosis of the heart), especially extracts of the endocrine glands (hormone therapy). The above quotation from Agrippa reminds us of the saying of Mephistopheles in Goethe's *Faust,*

Like to like [similia similibus], when one is sick, foot heals foot; And so with all the members.[51]

Much the same can be found in the instructions for animal magnetism:

In order to specially strengthen the lower extremities of a person, it is necessary for the healthy individual and the patient to put the soles of their feet together for a while; to strengthen the arms, they must clench their hands in such a way that the fingertips of the one lie in the hand of the other. By sitting in the [healthy person's] lap, the upper part of the thigh and the genitals are strengthened, and by placing themselves back to back the kidneys are strengthened.[52]

---

[51] J. W. v. Goethe, *Faust,* Part 2, Act I, Scene 6.

[52] Carl Buttenstedt, *Die Übertragung der Nervenkraft: Ansteckung durch Gesundheit* [The Transference of Nervous Energy: Infection by Health], Rüdersdorf/Berlin, n.d., 97.

I thought it important to make this slight digression, because it is where animal magnetism can usefully find a place in domestic medicine. Agrippa continues:

> *Thus if we wish to operate with some property or power, we have to look for animals . . . in which the property dwells to an unusual degree. And we must take from them the part in which the desired property or power is most active. If, for example, we wish to arouse love, we must seek an animal that is conspicuous for love. Among these are the dove, the sparrow, the swallow, and the wagtail. From these creatures we must take the parts or members where the instinct for love chiefly resides. Such parts are the heart, the testicles, the womb, the male member, the seed. . . . However, this has to be done during the mating season of the creatures, for then they are exceptionally useful for causing love.*

TENZEL said something similar a hundred and twenty years later. DURTAL muses:

> *On the other hand, Dr. Charles-Edouard BROWN-SEQUARD (1817–1894) rejuvenated frail old people and invigorated the impotent with extracts from the organs of rabbits and guinea-pigs. Who knows whether those elixirs of life, those magic love potions, sold by witches for sexual weakness or inactivity, were not composed of the same or similar substances?*[53]

As it happens, I can produce compelling evidence for the truth of this conjecture:

> *The coven met in Riepe on Christmas night 1542 in the kitchen of Frerich Dayen Warf. The said witches were assembled there in the devil's name, because their pubic hair had been shaved off . . . but in order to provoke*

---

[53] Joris K. Huysmans, *Tief unten*, Potsdam, 1921, 200.

their lust . . . having mutilated the bulls or stallions of their neighbors . . . they threw the parts into the cauldron. After dancing round it three or five times and giving it a stir, they sat down at the table and drank the hellish brew.[54]

The former Schwarzburg court physician Dr. Andreas TENZEL gave the following account of organotherapy in 1629:

Likewise a very useful prescription for enabling impotent husbands to do their duty to their wives, is the pizzle of a stag shot in rut, powdered and mixed with castor, or else the sperm itself sprinkled with pepper, dried, and then compounded with musk, ambergris, and Peruvian balsam.[55]

A therapy related to Organotherapy is *Isopathy* (Greek: *isos* = like, *pathos* = suffering), which aims to cure like with like, or a diseased organ with its "organ specific" product. It is clear from the Edda that the basic isopathic law was known to the old Teutons. In the section called "Loddfafnismâl," Woden teaches the Lodfafner that the earth force cures intoxication "as the biter the bite."[56] When in China someone is bitten by a rabid dog, a few dog hairs are bound into the wound. In India, the animal is killed and the victim is given its raw liver to eat.[57] A well-known old Knowledge Book advises us to crush the scorpion on the wound it causes.[58]

---

[54] Hermann Lübbing, *Friesische Sagen* [Frisian Tales], Jena, 1928, 174.

[55] Andreas Tenzel, *Medicina diastatica od. in die Ferne würkende Arzney-Kunst* [Medicina Diastatica or the Art of Remote-Acting Medicine], Leipzig & Hof, 1753, 101; Tenzel's book was translated into English by Ferdinando Parkhurst and published in London in 1653 under the title *Medicina Diastatica or Sympatheticall Mumie . . . Teaching the Magneticall cure of Diseases at Distance, etc.* The remedy itself is given on p. 74 but, oddly enough, the translation omits to say what it is supposed to cure! For "castor" Parkhurst has "the Oyle of Beavers-stone." The more modern term "castor" does, in fact, refer to a medical substance obtained from beaver: it does not mean "castor oil" here. Tr. note.].

[56] Hans von Wolzogen, *Die Edda*. Leipzig n.d., Reclam No. 781–784, 185.

[57] G. W. Surya, *Homöopathie, Isopathie, Biochemie* [Homeopathy, Isopathy, Biochemistry], Berlin-Pankow, 1923, 140–141.

[58] Anonymous, *Hundert Acht und Dreyssig gantz Neu-entdeckte Geheimnüsse etc. (Siebenundvierzigstes Stück)* [One Hundred and Thirty-Eight Altogether New-Discovered Secrets, etc. (Article Forty-Seven)] Frankfurt/Main, 1717, 49–50.

PARACELSUS (1493–1541) takes up what our author says and develops it: "Heart to heart, lungs to lungs, spleen to spleen. Not the spleen of sows, not the brain of sows to the brain of humans, but another human brain."[59] Thus he is prescribing an Ison of the same kind, not something alien!

In the opinion of the Zulus: "If one appropriates, in simple or in compound form, any substance, no matter what, one also appropriates the energy bound up in this substance. To benefit the eyes, the substance of the eye must be used. One might simply take a human or animal eye and eat it, or one might prepare a medicine from it . . . in this way remedies can be found for every conceivable ailment. Lung tissue helps in pulmonary disease, ear tissue in deafness. Wherever there is some incapacity, the cure can be found in tissue from the human or animal organ possessing the capacity required."[60] Furthermore, if a suspension of cells taken from a human organ is injected into an animal, a serum is produced in the animal's blood that regenerates and vitalizes human organs of the same type.[61]

---

[59] Paracelsus: *Labyrinthus medicorum,* chapter 9, § 43.

[60] Gustav Asmus, *Die Zulu* [The Zulus], Essen, 1939, 31.

[61] F. Wiedermann, *Die Kunst alt zu werden* [The Art of Growing Old], 1962. Other books that may be of interest are my *Rosicrucian Notebook,* Weiser, 1992; and the following titles in German: Dr. Ernst Busse, *Isopathia externa et interna* [Isopathy, External and Internal], Ulm/Donau, 1956; Dr. Ernst Consentius, *Meister Johann Dietz erzählt sein Leben* [Master Johann Dietz Tells the Story of his Life], Ebenhausen b. Munich, 1915, 67, 324; Prof. Gustav Jaeger, *Gleich und ähnlich* [Equal and Similar], Stuttgart, 1891; Jaeger, *Selbstarznei und Heilmagnetismus* [Self-Treatment and Animal Magnetism], Stuttgart, 1908, 36 f; Ernst Jünger, *Strahlungen III* [Radiations III], DTV No. 345, 246–247, Entry Sept. 12, 1945; Prof. Fritz Lickint, *Organismotherapie,* Jena, 1953; Phanegg *Nos maîtres: Le Dr. Papus* [Our Teachers: Dr. Papus], Paris, 1909, 74 f; Schrödter *Isopathie in "Vom Hundertsten ins Tausendste"* [Isopathy in "One Thing and Another"], Freiburg, 1940–1941, 149 f; G. W. Surya, *Homöopathie, Isopathie, Biochemie, Jatrochemie und Elektrohomöopathie* [Homeopathy, Biochemistry, Iatrochemistry, and Electrohomeopathy], Lorch/Württemberg, 1936.

OBJECTS AS CONVEYORS OF
CHARACTER TRAITS
(Chapter XVI)

It is said that the person who puts on the dress or blouse of a whore, or keeps the mirror into which she used to look every day, will become impudent, bold, shameless, and lascivious.

In order to make the correctness of this dictum (or even its probability) more apparent to the modern mind, it may helpful to look at some related topics. In the Acts of the Apostles 19: 12 we read that, in Ephesis, handkerchiefs or aprons were brought to the sick from the body of the apostle Paul "and the diseases departed from them, and the evil spirits went out of them."

The Swedish pastor, Friedrich August BOLTZIUS (1836–1910) successfully revived this apostolic, or early Christian, form of healing; for which reason it has been given the name of "Boltzianism." Underwear, especially when made of wool—but not of insulating silk—is a good "Od-carrier"[62] and becomes impregnated with surplus energy from the healer's body. But more than that: "The French researcher Prof. Hector DURVILLE (1849–1923) was driven to the conclusion by experiments revealing an effective universal magnetism, which he called vital force or life magnetism when found in the human body, that "in the human organism it is even determined by the moral quality of the individual"—that is to say by his or her purity."[63] This considered opinion was shared on the basis of personal experience by many noted magnetizers.[64]

We find Oskar KORSCHELT (1841–1940), professor of agriculture and inventor of an apparatus for collecting cosmic rays (a "solar etheric radiation apparatus") as a partial substitute for "human magnetism," thinking along the same lines when he sees the possibility of a mutual infection of character during

---

[62] Schrödter, *Präsenzwirkung*.

[63] Dr. Alfr. Strauß & G. W. Surya, *Theurgische Heilmethoden* [Theurgic Methods of Treatment], Lorch/Württemberg, 1936, 24; Hector Durville, *Die Physik des Animal-Magnetismus (Animismus)* [The Physics of Animal Magnetism (Animism)], Leipzig, 1912, 26.

[64] Friedr. Kallenberg, *Offenbarungen des siderischen Pendels* [Revelations of the Sidereal Pendulum], Diessen vor Munich, 1921, 29 f.

magnetic treatments (this was formerly designated *neurogamy*—Greek for nerve marriage!): "Not only the vital force of the healer, but also the healer's character, is communicated to the patient, and conversely the character of the patient flows into the healer."[65]

This is the reason for the dictum of Philipp MÜH of Stuttgart (1870–1946), who imparted vital force by the laying on of hands: "For the profession of magnetizer a good character is indispensable."[66] The widely held opinion that "if the flower she wears wither's she's a flirt,"[67] which I regard as quite possibly true, could easily be checked. Agrippa himself says a few pages further on (chapter XVIII): "The olive tree is so incompatible with a whore that, if it is planted by the latter, it will either remain unfruitful or wither away." Moral infection, which naturally enough is passed on most strongly by underclothing, can also be conveyed by less intimate items that are used every day by the immoral person, also by items held for a fairly long time in the hands. Handglasses come into this category for two reasons in particular: the undoubted existence of ocular rays,[68] and the peculiar effect of mercury-coated mirrors on sensitive persons.[69]

A very impressive picture is painted by the English adept Dion FORTUNE (1901–1946) of the influence of an article of

---

[65] Oskar Korschelt, *Die Nutzbarmachung der lebendigen Kraft des Äthers I. d. Heilkunst, Landwirtschaft und Technik* [The Utilization of the Living Force of the Ether in Medicine, Agriculture and Technical Science], Bad Schmiedeberg and Leipzig, n.d., 72 (ca. 1891); Schrödter, *Präsenzwirkung,* 125.

[66] Philipp Müh, *Psychische Gewalten: Angewandte Geheimwissenschaften* [Psychic Powers: Applied Secret Sciences], Lorch/Württemberg, 1911, 51.

[67] James Joyce, *Ulysses,* Bodley Head, London, 1960, 328.

[68] Dr. A. Keller, *Magnetismus—die Urheilkraft des menschen* [Magnetism—Humanity's Primal Healing Power], Cademario, 1959, 24; Anton Memminger, *Hakenkreuz und Davidstern (Volkstümliche Einführung i. d. Geheimwissenschaften)* [Swastika and Star of David: A Popular Introduction to the Occult Sciences], Würzburg, 1922, 221 f; Charles Russ, "An instrument that is set in motion by vision or the proximity of the human body," in *The Lancet,* London, 1921, 7.30.1921, p.222/8.6.1921, p. 308/8.13.1921, p. 361 f. Schrödter, *Präsenzwirkung,* 16–17, 77; Dr. Voeller, "Neue Anschauungen über Hypnose, Suggestion und Telepathie" [New Views on Hypnosis, Suggestion and Telepathy] in *Ztschr. f. Heilmagnetismus,* No. 8, November, 1926, 58 f; Dr. Biek, "Kann Hypnose heilen?" ["Can Hypnosis Cure?"] *Neustadt* (Weinstraße), 1957, 35–36; Anonymous, "Augenstrahlen werden gemessen" [Ocular rays have been measured], in *Ztrbl. f. Okkultismus,* Leipzig, 1932, 232, 249 f.

[69] Dr. Karl von Reichenbach, *Wer ist sensitiv, wer nicht?* [Who is Sensitive and Who Not?], Leipzig, 1920, 8; § 18.

clothing belonging to an "extremely psychoactive" (not to mention egocentric) "personality"[70] on a sensitive: "It was too cold to walk in the garden unprotected, so she [Veronica Mainwaring] took from its peg the old trench coat in which LUCAS had wrapped her when he brought her down from London, and clad in this garment, she went out into the woods. . . . Clothes are strange things, they seem to absorb something of the personality of their wearers. VERONICA found herself enveloped in the mental atmosphere that LUCAS always emanated. . . ."[71]

COMPATIBILITY OF CERTAIN PLANTS AND ANIMALS
(Chapter XVII)

The vine is compatible with the elm and the poppy; olives and myrtles and olives and fig-trees are also compatible.

This is what a modern investigator of arcane matters, Johan August STRINDBERG (1849–1912) has to say about happy "marriages" between plants: Certain plants thrive in each other's company, others do not, although one cannot exactly say why. Since Roman times, the vine has always been "wedded" to the elm, to which it looks for support, and even more to the Spanish chestnut (as in Savoy), and to the poplar mulberry tree (as in Lombardy). . . . Onions have been planted in the rose parks of Provence, in order to enhance the scent of the roses. If the onion is regarded as a sort of lily, this would quite well explain the sympathy between the rose and the lily.[72]

---

[70] A technical term coined by the medical hypnotist Dr. Franz (Ferenc) VÖLGYESI, (born 1895). It occurs in his *Mindealélek* (Budapest, 1941) issued in German as *Die Seele ist alles* [The Soul is All], Zürich, 1948, 25–26).

[71] Dion Fortune, *The Demon Lover*, York Beach, ME, Samuel Weiser, 1972, pp. 150–151.

[72] August Strindberg, *Ein Blaubuch* (A Blue Book), Munich, 1920, 370.

A knowledge of plant affinities is vitally important to gardeners who wish to obtain the optimum yields.[73] As far as fauna are concerned, AGRIPPA writes:

In the animal kingdom, friendship exists between the blackbird and the thrush, between the crow and the heron, between peacocks and pigeons, between turtle-doves and parrots.

There are also epizoic partnerships—such as those between the crocodile and the crocodile-bird, the shark and the pilot-fish.

HEALING INSTINCT IN ANIMALS
(Chapter XVII)

Some animals possess a medical instinct. If the tortoise is bitten by a poisonous snake, it heals itself by eating origanum; the stork also helps itself with origanum when eating snakes. When the weasel intends to attack the basilisk, it eats rue, from which we can draw the conclusion that origanum and rue are effective anti-dotes to poisons. In this way human beings have learned many remedies for diseases and a whole series of [other] things from animals.

Although Agrippa cites more examples, these are enough to illustrate our theme. I also must limit the number of modern instances, while pointing out that there are many more that could be mentioned. "The founder of electrohomeopathy, Count Cesare MATTEI (1809–1896), observed while strolling in the environs of his Moorish mountain castle not far from the small town of Riola (between Bologna and Florence), a mangy dog belonging to a neighboring estate. MATTEI noticed how the dog, "in consequence of its healing instincts," frequently searched the

---

[73] H. Zörnitz, *Das Geheimnis einer glückl. Pflanzenehe* [The Secret of a Happy Plant Marriage], Wuppertal–Barmen, 1946.

mountain forest for certain herbs, and eagerly devoured them until it had cured itself of its virulent disease.

On making this observation, MATTEI gathered these herbs and discovered that they were also capable of healing in human beings eruptions and other diseases designated as "scrofulous."[74] "Several years ago the colony of crows in Allgäu expanded. They flew in huge flocks to their roosts, covered the fields, nested, multiplied, etc. But they were not wary of the poisonous bait that was laid—with some success—in huge quantities for them at that time. However, the poisoned birds settled in places where loam and clay were exposed and water was also present. They ate the soil and drank the water alternately in large amounts until they were well again."[75] "Cows that normally avoided the leaves of the poisonous meadow-saffron, ate them when the latter were frozen."[76]

The way in which we can make practical use of the fine senses and instinctive sense of smell possessed by animals is shown by the example of the naturopathic doctor Prof. Gustav JAEGER (1832–1917), whose dog sniffed out for him that pure wool is better than half-wool;[77] or that of the Argentinian research institute which employed white cabbage butterflies to discover plants with similar chemical constituents.[78]

Someone who is training to be a doctor of medicine (*Izinyanga zamakambi*) among the Zulus also acquires a knowledge of the medicinal properties of plants by observing the activities of every creature and drawing his conclusions from them. "Thus one of these doctors once saw two mambas (snakes) fighting with and inflicting bite wounds on one another. When they finally tired of fighting, he noticed how each snake looked for a certain herb, bit off a piece, and chewed and swallowed it. And this was how he found an antidote to the deadly bite of the mamba."[79]

---

[74] G. W. Surya, *Homöopathie, Isopathie, Biochemie, Jatrochemie und Elektrohomöopathie* [Homeopathy, Isopathy, Biochemistry, Iatrochemistry, and Electrohomeopathy], Berlin-Pankow, 1923, 183–184.

[75] Gustav Schenk, *Schatten der Nacht* [Shadow of the Night], Hanover, 1948, 127–128.

[76] J. Schier, *Biologische Erfahrungsheillehre* [Biological Empirical Therapeutic Knowledge], Stuttgart, 1941.

[77] Willy Schrödter, "Tiere als Heiler" [Animals as Healers] in *Natur & Kultur*, Issue 2, 14. Munich-Solln, 1958, 101; Surya, *Homöopathy*, etc., 146–147; Gustav Jaeger, *Gleich und ähnlich* [Equal and Similar], Stuttgart, 1891.

[78] Schrödter, as above, 19,

[79] Gustav Asmus, *Die Zulu* [The Zulus], Essen, 1939, 102.

GEM THERAPY
(Chapter XVIII)

Gem therapy, or healing by the use of gems, can be traced from the didactic poem "Lithiká" of the Greek singer of incantations (French: *enchanteur*) and originator of the "Orphic mysteries,"[80] ORPHEUS of Pempleia in Thrace (born 1399 B.C.), right down to a gem therapy book written by a well-known pharmacologist and published in 1955.[81] Agrippa has this to say:

> *The sapphire is antagonistic to plague-ulcers, feverishness, and eye diseases; the amethyst to intoxication; the jasper to hemorrhages . . .; the emerald to lasciviousness; the agate to poisons; coral to melancholy and stomach-ache; the topaz to passions such as avarice, gluttony and all kinds of debauchery.*

To those who refuse offhand to credit any healing power to gems because of their alleged power to remove moral as well as physical ailments, we would say that our modern homeopathy makes and justifies the same claim.[82] In regard to some of the stones mentioned by Agrippa, Dr. Franz HARTMANN (1838–1912) has successfully prescribed wearing coral necklaces for depression; modern medicine has been forced to admit the calming influence of the amethyst in hysteria and the removal of acute neuralgia when the forehead is stroked with it; and Dr. Fred R. MORRISON of Kentucky prescribed topaz bangles for soothing the nerves.[83]

Around the turn of the century, a Westerwald peasant's wife would place a piece of quartz in her kitchen, and possibly hang a string of tiny quartz stones round the neck of the little child lying in its cot, because this particular stone attracted to

---

[80] Lutz Kricheldorf, "Orpheus und der Orphismus" [Orpheus and Orphism] in *Blätter für Anthroposophie*, No. 1, January, Basel, 1960, 17 f.

[81] Prof. Hermann Führner, *Lithotherapie: Hist. Studien üb. d. med. Verwendung der Edelsteine* [Gem Therapy: Historical Studies of the Use of Precious Stones in Medicine], Ulm, 1955.

[82] Jean Pierre Gallavardin, *Homöopathische Beeinflussung von Charakter, Trunksucht und Sexualtrieb* [The Homeopathic Effect on Character, Dipsomania and Sexual Desire], selected, translated, and edited by Dr. Hans Triebel, Ulm, 1958.

[83] Willy Schrödter, "Lithotherapie" [Gem Therapy] in *Erfahrungsheilkunde*, No. 5, May, Ulm, 1957, 221 f.

itself the unavoidable dampness from the stove and prevented the onset of bronchial attacks. Up to this point we have been considering the wearing, placing, or application of precious stones. Their modern medical use in solution is seen in the prescription for cramp of a volatile oil extracted from amber.[84] With succinic acid (part of the citric acid cycle) the effects of LSD are aborted and the facial swelling in schizophrenic seizures is reduced (Otto F. Beer). No less a person than Prof. Leo Cunibert MOHL-BERG (1878–1963), wearer of the Grand Distinguished Service Cross of the Federal Republic, maintains that: "It is not a piece of superstition when Swiss mothers hang amber beads round the necks of their teething children, but is a measure based on the fact that amber—like brass and coal—exhibits a very high (six-fold) degree of penetrability by radiation."[85]

Indian medicine—at least in the treatment of sick Maharajahs—revels even today in medicines compounded of specific precious stones and real pearls.[86] The well-known dowser, Count Bernhard MATUSCHKA-TOPPOLCZAN (1886-1966) of Spaettgen, used to prepare "gem-irradiation capsules" which afforded relief to many sufferers.[87]

---

[84] Elizabeth and A. M. Villiers-Pachinger, *Amulette und Talismane u. andere geheime Dinge* [Amulets and Talismans and Other Esoteric Matters], Munich, 1927, 21.

[85] L. C. Mohlberg, *Briefe an Tschü* [Letters to Tschü], Ulm (Donau), 1959, 296 f. ("Candi").

[86] Detailed information on Indian gem therapy may be found in *Gem Therapy* by Dr. Benoytosh Bhattacharyya, revised and enlarged by A. K. Bhattacharyya, published by Firma K. L. Mukhopadhyay, Calcutta, 1971. The book warns that gems must not be used indiscriminately, and tells the story of a man who started wearing a "powerful" ruby ring. "For the first three months nothing happened. But at the end of this period one day he developed very high temperature . . . there was a collapse with profuse perspiration . . . his lower limbs were paralysed . . . The patient was asked to remove the ring from his person and from the house he was occupying . . . his two-year-old temperature vanished within 24 hours. As the ruby was not there to impart heat to the organism, the old temperature could not be sustained and the fever was off" (loc. cit. pp. 15–16). Tr. note.

[87] Eberhard Maria Körner, *Wege zum Licht* [Pathway to the Light], Garm.-Partenkirchen, 1962, 233–234.

INCOMPATIBILITY OF CERTAIN
PLANTS AND ANIMALS
(Chapter XVIII)

*Ants are averse to marjoram . . . which is also inimical
to spiders and salamanders. There is such discord between it and the cabbage that they destroy one another.
. . . Among birds the crows and the screech-owls are
continually at war.*

These few examples are all we can quote now, although Agrippa gives many more—not without mixing fact and fable, as
was usual with the writers of his day. To the example of the
aversion of ants to marjoram, I would add that emmets (ants)
cannot endure the smell of tomatoes, chervil, elder leaves, and
lavender flowers. Further instances will be found in my *Plant
Secrets*.[88]

When put into practice, biological pest control is extremely useful to the gardener, which is why we have made this
particular quotation from Agrippa. When the latter says that
marjoram and cabbage destroy one another, we are reminded
that even in antiquity it was realized that cabbages and vines are
deadly enemies. Dr. Gustav JAEGER (1832–1917) has verified
this opinion (which has been expressed in every century) in his
own garden![89]

An old scholar says quite acutely: "Whoever wants to
have beautiful gardens that are productive or fruitful, must carefully note which things grow well together and which do not; for
one plant often takes away or injures the strength of another."[90]
This is a further hint to gardeners.

---

[88] Willy Schrödter, *Pflanzen-Geheimnisse* [Plant Secrets], 21 f (chapter on plants as a pro-
tection against pests).
[89] Gustav Jaeger, *Entdeckung der Seele* [Discovery of the Soul], Leipzig, 1880, 335.
[90] Levinus Lemnius, *Occulta naturae miracula: Das ist, Wunderbarliche Geheimnisse der
Natur, etc.* [Nature's Hidden Wonders: Curious Secrets of Nature, etc.], 4th edition, improved and enlarged by Dr. Jacob Horst, Frankfurt/Main, 1672, 469.

ANIMALS AND THE DOCTRINE OF SIGNATURES
(Chapter XVIII)

Sheep avoid the celery-leaved crowfoot as deadly; and, what is more amazing, nature has imprinted the image of this death-dealer on the sheep's liver, on which one can see a lifelike representation of the said plant.

The reviver of occult medicine, G. W. SURYA (Demeter Georgiewicz-Weitzer, 1837–1914) offers us another example of the *signatura rerum:* "The stomach is governed by the fire principle (it 'cooks' the food) and it is amazing to see under the microsocpe that the mucous membrane of the stomach is an exact image of a row of flames, just as (similarly though in another connection) the Hebrew letter *Shin* (שsh), as a symbol of fire, resembles flames."[91] I must leave these two sources responsible for their assertions—which are easily checked. As a so-called *Lusus naturae* (Latin, "freak of nature") it has been recorded (but not explained!) that a moulting mark presented a realistic picture of a crouching rabbit on the inside of a rabbit skin.[92]

AILUROPHOBIA (ALLERGY TO CATS)
(Chapter XIX)

There are people who so loathe the sight of a cat that they cannot look at one without shuddering.

The word *ailurophobia* (Greek: *ailouros* = a cat, *phobos* = fear) is the technical term for this psychopathic idiosyncrasy. A classic case is that of the ailurophobe who went into convulsions and fell

---

[91] G. W. Surya, *Der Traumdenker* [The Dream Philosopher], Ludwig Aub., Munich, 1920; Willy Schrödter, *Tier-Geheimnisse* [Animal Secrets], p. 90 (chapter on Animals and the Doctrine of Signatures). [Another traditional view is that the shape of the letter Shin "resembles a molar, which crushes food with its three sharply edged cusps." Rabbi Michael L. Munk, *The Wisdom of the Hebrew Alphabet,* Mesorah Publications, New York, 1983, p. 213. T̲r̲. n̲o̲t̲e̲.]

[92] Dr. Eugen Georg, "Die Zahl wird lebendig" [Numbers are Alive] in *Das Dritte Auge,* vol. 8, Klagenfurt, May, 1934, 143–149.

unconscious on the ground floor of a house due to the presence of a family of cats on the top floor, even though he did not know they were there and could not see, hear, or smell them. When carried into the garden, he immediately recovered, but suffered from further paroxysms on re-entering the room.[93]

A celebrity who was also an ailurophobe was Napoleon Bonaparte (1769–1821). Allergies of this sort even concern people belonging to a certain class, as we learn further on (in chapter LV): "Often, if a prostitute is concealed in a very big house, someone will sense her presence without knowing the slightest about it. History tells of an Egyptian named Heraiscus, a divinely enlightened man, who could recognize unchaste women . . . even from a distance, and would suffer from a severe headache."

TASTE PERVERSION
(Chapter XIX)

Albertus Magnus mentions seeing a girl in Cologne who literally hunted for spiders because she liked the taste of them.

The authority quoted by author—Albert the Great (1193–1280), count of Bollstädt, who became a Dominican, scientist, theologian, philosopher, and bishop of Regensburg (being surnamed "Doctor universalis" because of his varied talents), was canonized in 1931, and can be regarded as a reliable observer. Besides, his testimony has the support of more recent cases. For example, the astronomer Joseph-Jérôme Le Français DE LALANDE (1732–1807) used to carry an expensive-looking box on his person, and would horrify his companions every now and then by taking a fat spider out of it and putting it in his mouth to eat with every sign of enjoyment—just as if it were a piece of candy.[94]

---

[93] Carl Alex. Ferd. Kluge, *Versuch einer Darstellung des animalischen Magnetismus als Heilmittel* [Provisional Account of Animal Magnetism as a Means of Cure], Berlin, 1815, 244, § 205; Carl Gustav Carus, *Über Lebenmagnetismus und die magischen Wirkungen überhaupt* [Animal Magnetism and Magical Operations in General], Reprint of 1857, Basel, 1925, 82, 115.

[94] Willy Schrödter, *Tier-Geheimnisse* [Animal Secrets], 236.

IMMUNITY TO POISON
(Chapter XIX)

Avicenna relates that in his days there lived a man who was avoided by all poisonous creatures; any of which that accidentally bit him died as a result, while he himself was not harmed.

The words "as a result" must refer to poison to which he had systematically inured himself that was present in the man's body. Such habituation to poison is named "mithridatizing" for Mithridates VI (132–63), surnamed Eupator, Dionysios, also The Great, King of Pontus (from 120), because he is the most notable person known to practice it. His name means "Sun father." AVICENNA (Abu Ali al Hussein Ibn Sina, 980–1037) was an Iranian physician and philosopher, whose "Canon" formed medical opinion in the Middle Ages.

A contemporary example is that of a worker in a chemical factory in South America who was in daily contact with potassium iodide and was completely saturated with it. On the way home in 1956, he was bitten by a rattlesnake, which died within a few minutes of the poison to which his own body had gradually become immune over the years; he himself was not harmed by the venom of the viper.[95]

In this connection, mention should be made of the Indian "poison-maidens" (*visakanya*) or "poison-women" (*visangana*), who were systematically inured from the cradle to monk's-hood (*Aconitum ferox* or *napellus*) and whose love-bites were deadly to those who were not immune. Such poison-carrying courtesans were regularly used as weapons by the ruling classes.[96] The immunity of fakirs and yogis to poison is well-documented.[97]

---

[95] The Saarbrücken "Volksstimme" carried a broadly similar news item three years earlier (No. 230 of 10.5.1953) under the heading "Da staunte die Klapperschlange" [The Rattlesnake had a Nasty Shock]. According to this version, the person concerned was a Mr. Hiroc GOMEZ, a scientific assistant in a Brazilian botanical institute, and the chemical was sodium cyanide.

[96] Dr. Siegfr. Seligmann, *Die Zauberkraft des Auges und das Berufen* [The Magic Power of the Eye and the Vocation], Hamburg, 1922, 275 f.

[97] Major Francis Yeats-Brown, *Ist Yoga für dich?* [Is Yoga for You?], Berlin, n.d..

THE AURA
(Chapter XX)

The hyena acts by the force of its whole being in such a way that dogs are silenced when they come in contact with its shadow.

If the sun is not shining, the hyena cannot throw a "shadow"! Clearly, therefore, it is the "Odic shadow" to which reference is being made in this "personal influence" of an animal. An interesting reference to the shadow occurs in "The Acts of the Apostles" (ch. 5: 14–15): "And believers were the more added to the Lord, multitudes both of men and women. Insomuch that they brought forth the sick into the streets, and laid them on beds and couches, that at least the shadow of Peter passing by might overshadow some of them."

Agrippa has something in the same vein a little earlier (chapter XVIII):

The olive tree is said to be so incompatible with a whore that, if it is planted by one, either it remains unfruitful or else it withers.

The "Irish chronometrist with the X-ray eyes," James JOYCE (1882–1941), repeats the popular opinion: "If the flower she wears withers, she's a flirt."[98] One thing is certain: "some plants react badly when worn by persons with injurious radiations. . . . In rooms that are full of evil human aura[99] they wilt and fade. If they are worn in the button-hole of someone who is inimical to them, it is amazing how quickly they lose their scent and shape, and how soon they droop."[100]

In contrast, we have practical people with "lucky hands" (Germany), gardeners with "green thumbs" (England), and strokers with "golden hands" (China). Those who are very feeble and those who are insane have (almost) no aura; figuratively

---

[98] James Joyce, *Ulysses.*
[99] Willy Schrödter, *Präsenzwirkung*, 126, 128, 142.
[100] Dr. Fr. Markus Huebner, *Menschen als Arznei und Gift* [People as Medicine and Poison], Kampen (Sylt), 1934, 38.

speaking they cast no shadow. (Cf. "Peter Schlemihl" by Adal-bert von CHAMISSO, 1781-1838). At the other end of the scale there are the extremely "psychoactive" personalities described in the section on "Odic flames"!

THE "EVIL EYE"
(Chapter XX)

In Scythia and among the Illyrians there were women who—so it is said—could kill with an angry glance.

This is the "evil eye," to which reference has been made in every place and age. JESUS CHRIST called it a "knavish eye."[101] Modern Italians still speak of the *mal occhio* or *jettatura,* and its owners as *jettatore.* Charles LAFONTAINE (1803–1882), one of the most renowned French mesmerists of a hundred years ago, on more than one occasion killed small animals within a quarter of an hour by his gaze.[102] German magnetizers endeavored some decades ago to demonstrate by simple means the existence of the *émission pesante,* or "ponderable emission" from the human eye[103, 104] and the Englishman Charles RUSS and the German Dr. Walter VOELLER (1893–1954) have detected ocular rays with instruments.[105]

---

[101] Matthew 6: 22–23. [W.S. follows Luther's version. The King James version has "If thine eye be evil." But David Stern comments: ". . . in Judaism 'having a good eye,' an *'ayin tovah,* means 'being generous,' and 'having a bad eye,' an *'ayin ra'ah,* means 'being stingy.' That this is the correct interpretation is confirmed by the context . . ." David H. Stern, *Jewish New Testament Commentary,* p. 32. JNTP, Inc., Clarksville, 1992. Tr. note.]

[102] Charles Lafontaine, *L'Art de magnétiser ou Magnétisme* [Magnetism, or the Art of Magnetizing], Paris, 1860, 331, f.

[103] Johann Schabenberger, *Das Wesen des Heilmagnetismus* [The Nature of Magnetism], Munich, 1906, 12 f.

[104] Max Breitung, *Der Heilmagnetismus i. d. Familie* [Mesmerism in the Family], Leipzig, 1924, 42; Schrödter, *Grenzwissenschaftliche Versuche* [Paranormal Experiments], 55.

[105] Charles Russ, "An instrument that is set in motion by vision or the proximity of the human body," in *The Lancet,* 7.30.1921, 8.6.1921, 8.13.1921, London 222, 308, 361 f; Dr. Hch. Biek, *Kann Hypnose heilen?* [Can Hypnosis Heal?], Neustadt (Weinstraße), 1957, 35–36; Anton Memminger, *Hakenkreuz und Davidstern: Volkstümliche Einführung i. d.*

Today the phenomenon of the "evil eye" has been given the scientific name psychobolia (Greek: *psyche* = soul; *ballo* = to throw); and the head of the Parapsychological Society in Athens has written a monograph on the subject.[106] In the 65th chapter of his book, Agrippa returns to this theme:

> *When sorcerers wish to do harm, they are able to entrance people in a very pernicious way by means of a fixed gaze. And Avicenna, Aristotle, Algazel and Galen all agree. . . . Now a power lies in the vapors of the eye that can bewitch and infect those who are close by, as the basilisk and cockatrice kill people with their glance, and many women in Scythia and Illyria and Triballia were able to kill whoever they stared at fiercely.*

The "fixed gaze" is used in hypnosis. "Vapors" would be called emanations or rays today. That many animals are able to hypnotize other animals (and even humans!) I have shown elsewhere.[107] Aristotle, Avicenna, and Galen are probably familiar names to most readers; ALGAZEL is Abu Hamid ibn Muhammad al-GHAZALI (1059–1111), the most important Islamic philosopher and mystic.

---

105 con't.

Geheimwissenschaften [The Swastika and the Star of David: A Popular Introduction to the Occult Sciences], Würzburg, 1922, 221–222; Walter Voeller, "Neue Anschauungen üb. Hypnose, Suggestion und Telepathie" [New Views on Hypnosis, Suggestion, and Telepathy], in *Ztschr. f. Heilmagnetismus*, No. 8, November, 1926, Halle/Saale, 58 f; Dr. Albert Leprince, *Des Radiations cosmiques aux ondes humaines* [From Cosmic Rays through Human Waves], Dangles: Paris, 1948, 148; Willy Schrödter, *Präsenzwirkung*, 16–17.

[106] Dr. Angelos Tanagras, *Le Destin et la Chance* [Destiny and Chance], Société des Recherches psychiques, rue Aristoteles, 67, Paris ca. 1946.

[107] Willy Schrödter, *Tier-Geheimnisse* [Animal Secrets] (section on "Animals as Hypnotists"), 115–121; see also Dr. Siegfried Seligmann, *Der böse Blick und Verwandtes* [The Evil Eye and Associated Matters]. Berlin, 1910; Seligmann, *Die Zauberkraft des Auges und das Berufen* [The Magic Power of the Eye, etc.], Hamburg, 1922; Willy Schrödter, "Der böse Blick" [The Evil Eye] in *Die Andere Welt*, vol. 7, July, Freiburg, 1963, 538–539.

THE RESURRECTION BONE
(Chapter XX)

*In the human body there is a very small bone called
LUS by the Hebrews, which is the size of a pea, and is
incorruptible, also it is not capable of being damaged
by fire, but always remains unhurt. According to Jewish tradition, when the dead are raised, our new bodies
will sprout from it as plants do from seeds. . . . However, these powers cannot be fathomed by the mind,
but have to be verified empirically.*

"ULS" lies in the region of the cross-bar.

From the venerable sacred literature of Judaism through the ana-
tomical books of the Renaissance, we find descriptions of the
"resurrection bone LUS." Caspar BAUHINUS (1691) located it in
the spine between the 18th vertebra and the thigh bone; HIER-
ONOYDUS MAGUS said it was in the skull; some identified it
with the coccyx, which MUHAMMAD (570–632) had stated was
indestructible, or with the coracoid process fused to the ventral
end of the scapula.[108] "But this Luz of the Kabbalah is identical
with the ULS of Egyptian lore, which is situated where spine
curves inward between the occiput and the shoulders. *Luz* in
Hebrew and *Uls* in ancient Egyptian both mean "inward curve"
or "bend" . . . this was seen as a favorable place for awakening

---

[108] Willy Schrödter, "Über den Heilmagnetismus" [Mesmerism] in *Mensch und Schicksal*,
No. 9, Villach, 15th July, 1955, 11f.

the mental powers of a person. Numerous passages testify that the purpose of "Sa-stroking" was to arouse the inner life.[109] The only comment required is that "Sa-stroking" was a special biomagnetic manipulation.

APPROXIMATION
(Chapter XXI)

If, in griping pains, a live duck is placed on the abdomen, the illness will go but the duck will die.

So-called "sympathetic cure" has various ways of "transplanting" disease by applying suitable animals to oneself in some way. In every place and age, dogs and guinea-pigs have been the "disease attractants" par excellence; so it is surprising that our author, of all people, should take the ornamental, but otherwise little-used, duck as an example.

Here we shall confine our attention to dogs. Caius PLINIUS Secundus (called "The Elder") (23–79) advised laying young dogs on the chest and stomach for a period of several days, and then the illness would be transferred to them: "If they are dissected, the seat of the disease will be found in them!" The English Rosicrucian, Dr. Robert FLUDD (Robertus de Fluctibus, 1574–1637) describes how he transplanted gout into his sleeping dog, which suffered from it for sometime and—like its master before it—was unable to walk. Similar reports have been made by "the bright star of Denmark," Prof. Friedrich BARTHOLINUS (1616–1680), royal physician Pierre BOREL (Petrus Borellus, 1620–1689), and the inventor of "Hoffmann's drops," Dr. Friedrich HOFFMANN (1660–1742). Army surgeon, Dr. Carl Alexander Ferdinand KLUGE (1782–1844) recorded the successful treatment of cases of cramp. The entire ninth chapter of the

---

[109] Carl Kiesewetter, *Der Occultismus des Altertums* [The Occultism of Antiquity] (chapter on "Mesmerism in Ancient Egypt"), Leipzig, 1896; Fritz Lambert, "Vor 3000 Jahre. Hypnotismus und Elektrizität im alten Ägypten" [3000 Years Ago: Hypnotism and Electricity in Ancient Egypt], in *Sphinx*, January, Gera, 1888, 276 f.

eighth book of *Occulta Naturae Miracula* [Nature's Hidden Wonders] by Levinus LEMNIUS deals with "natural warming by living animals, and in particular by young puppies; so that, when they are laid on cold or weak members until the latter are well warmed, this warming not only strengthens a poor digestion but also eases the pain in rheumatic limbs. Of all animals, young puppies are the best for this purpose. The university professor of zoology, William MARSHALL (1845–1907) pointed out in 1894 how effective for pain was the animal heat of a dog: "If one is suffering from gout, one should let oneself be licked by a dog: the gout will disappear, but the dog will become lame." There used to be "gout dogs" in Mecklenburg that were laid on painful limbs during the hours of sleep for the cure of rheumatism, and even until quite recently no dog license was required for them! Not so long ago a case occurred in which a man suffering from rheumatism regularly transferred his ailment to his dogs, and most of them died as a result. He was known locally by the nickname *lou crebo tchi,* which in the *langue d'oc* means 'dog destroyer'."[110] "A person with bad nerves should play with a cat, and then the trouble will go."[111]

THINGS RULED BY THE MOON
(Chapter XXIV)

Things ruled by the moon (lunar things) are, among the elements, earth and then water, both sea-water and river-water, and all wetness, the sap of trees and the juices of animals, chiefly when white, as in albumen, fat, perspiration, mucus, and other bodily fluids. . . . Among metals silver is lunar . . ., cats are also lunar . . ., also blood and the monthly periods.

Water—Most obvious effect: the tides, which also occur in the atmosphere.

---

[110] Willy Schrödter, *Tier-Geheimnisse* [Animal Secrets], 81 f, (chapter on "Animals and Sympathetic Action").
[111] H. Schmidt, *Volksmedizinisches aus dem Kanton Glarus* [Folk Medicine from Glarus], Zürcher medizingeschichtliche Abhandlungen, III, 51, Zürich, 1924.

Earth—During ebb and flow, the solid surface of the continents is displaced by many feet.

The sap of trees—No Brazilian timber merchant will start cutting when the moon is waning in case the wood splinters. And we need to remember at this point that the influence of the moon is stronger in the tropics, because only there do its rays strike the earth vertically.

The juices of animals—In Argentina, meat that is exposed overnight to the rays of the moon turns an unpleasant color and has a disgusting smell. Fish in South Africa are even said to become poisonous in the same circumstances.

Human fluids—The secretion of uric acid depends on the age of the moon. The thyroid gland and goiter often become enlarged toward full moon and shrink toward the last quarter.

Lunar silver—Experiments performed by Anthroposophists on silver compounds reveal the dependence of these on the phases of the moon.

Cats—The poet and physician Hans CAROSSA (1878–1956) wrote: "When I stroke your forehead / I suddenly feel the moon," and with this verse underlined our author's opinion, which I myself have confirmed elsewhere.[112] The cat is a magnetic-mantic animal!

Monthly periods—Carl Gustav CARUS (1789–1869) has supplied useful information on this.[113]

I have been unable to verify the other correspondences mentioned by Agrippa in this chapter. A passing reference to the topic occurs in Book III, chapter 64:

> *Shell-fish, crabs, and oysters put on flesh when the moon is waxing but grow thinner when it is waning.*

---

[112] Willy Schrödter, *Tier-Geheimnisse* [Animal Secrets], 204, etc.
[113] C. G. CARUS, *Über Lebensmagnetismus, etc.* [Animal Magnetism, etc.], Basel, 1929.

This opinion has been handed down to us from the ancient Greek writers by GLOREZ[114] and TENZEL.[115] The Greeks maintained that the phenomenon probably had to do with reproductive activity (swelling of the gonads), an observation that has recently been confirmed by the English scientist FOX.[116]

INVISIBLE INKS
(Chapter XXXIV)

. . . just as the heat of the fire brings to light invisible letters that have been written in onion juice or milk, and just as the completely hidden letters written on a stone with goat's fat emerge and look as if they were carved as soon as the stone is dipped in vinegar. . . .

Brockhaus [a German reference work] has this to say under the above heading: "Dilute cobalt chloride; dilute acidic ferric chloride solution. The colorless writing made with the former turns red when heated, that made with the latter turns red when moistened with thiocyanic acid." Recipes for invisible ink abound in conjuring books.[117]

---

[114] Andreas Glorez, *Eröffnetes Wunderbuch, etc.* [An Open Wonder-Book, etc.], Regensburg & Stadtamhof, 1700.

[115] Andreas Tenzel, *Medicina diastatica,* Leipzig & Hof, 1753, 113 [English translation by Ferdinando PARKHURST, London, 1653. The passage in question reads: "Now let us speak of the *Moon,* with whom the bodies of *Oysters, Cockles,* and all shell Fish, do equally increase and decrease; etc." (p. 85). Tr. note].

[116] Proceedings of the SPR, vol. 175, London.

[117] Joe Labéro, *Wundermänner, ich enthülle eure Geheimnisse* [Miracle Workers, I Reveal Your Secrets], Berlin, 1933, 117.

THE HOMUNCULUS
(Chapter XXXVI)

There is a clever feat by which a human form can be produced in an egg placed under a brood-hen, as I myself have seen and know how to do. Magicians ascribe wonderful powers to a form such as this and call it the true Alraun.

As a supplement to this, we would refer to the Scottish physician Dr. William MAXWELL (1619–1669), the precursor of Dr. Franz Anton MESMER (1733–1815) and friend of the English defender of the Rosicrucians, Dr. Robert FLUDD. Maxwell took human blood, which the routine blood-letting of his day made so freely available, and allowed this to ferment, but he kept secret the critically important fermentation time. This is the "very special juice." "Put it under a hen to incubate. After the expiry of a certain time you will find an anthropoid mass, with which you can perform many wonders, and also a surrounding oil or fluid. Many wonders can be performed by means of the blood—if only you know how to use it correctly—but I prefer to pass them over in silence. Nevertheless, if you fully understand what has been said, and if you diligently study nature, you will be able to obtain the knowledge yourself."[118]

An intimation of what "wonders" may be expected from the use of blood is to be found in the so-called "powder of sympathy."[119]

---

[118] William Maxwell, *Medicina magnetica: Libri III, etc.* [Magnetic Medicine: Three Books, etc.], Frankfurt, 1678; *Drei Bücher der magnetischen Heilkunde* [Three Books of Magnetic Medicine], editor, Dr. Gg. Frank, Stuttgart, 1855, 185 f. *Magisch-Magnetische Heilkunde* [Magical Magnetic Medicine], Editor, E. Issberner-Haldane, Berlin, 1954, 82.

[119] Willy Schrödter, *Grenzwiss: Versuche* [Paranormal Researches], chapter on "The Powder of Sympathy," 247 ff.

AS ABOVE SO BELOW
(INFERIUS QUOD SUPERIUS)
(Chapter XXXVII)

The Academics, Hermes Trismegistus, the Brahmin Jarchas, and the Hebrew Kabbalists maintain that everything that is subject to generation and decay in the sublunar world, is also to be found in the celestial world—in a celestial fashion of course. They are also to be found in the spiritual world, where they are closer to perfection, and ultimately in the world of Archetypes, where they are most nearly perfect. In this series, each "below" corresponds to its "above," and through the latter it corresponds to the "highest" according to its nature. From the celestial world it receives the celestial virtue we call the quintessence, worldsoul, or middle nature; from the spiritual world, it receives a spiritual and animating strength and every qualitative supersensual power; finally, from the archetypal world, it receives, through these intermediate stages, the moving principle of all perfection. Therefore each thing in our world can be assigned to the stars, from these to their Intelligences, and from the latter to the Archetypes on which arrangement the whole of magic and all occult philosophy depends. . . . This attraction arising from the mutual agreement of things—the Above with the Below—was called sympathy by the Greeks . . . And so, if something below is set in motion, so is something above to which it corresponds, like the strings of a well-tuned lyre.

The Academics were scholars of PLATO (Aristokles, 427–347), and used to convene in a grove in Athens that once belonged to the hero Academus. HERMES TRISMEGISTOS (Greek, "Thrice great Hermes") is the Greek name for the Egyptian moon god THOTH and was equated with the Hellenic messenger of the gods HERMES [Mercury]. He was said to be the god of magicians and alchemists (alchemy is known as the "hermetic art"). His hermetic philsophy was formulated in hermetic books, which were passed on (in a so-called hermetic chain) by a series of initiates.

JARCHAS was a Brahmin who is understood to have instructed APPOLONIUS OF TYANA (10–90?) in Indian philosophy. Finally, the Kabbalah (Hebrew: "received tradition") is the Jewish secret doctrine that has been handed down from antiquity. It touches on the subjects of the magical properties of the divine names (*Shem*) and the metaphysical meaning of numbers (numerology). Its followers are called Kabbalists and their procedure is known as Kabbalism. Their main works are the Zohar (Hebrew: "Splendor") and the Sefer Yetzirah (Hebrew: "The Book of Creation"). According to the Kabbalah, there are four worlds:

1) Atziloth: the highest world, that of spiritual transcendence;
2) Briah: the world of ideas and intuitions;
3) Yetzirah: the world of astral (stellar) powers;
4) Asiah: the world of realization; that is to say our material world.

In chapter LXVIII, Agrippa briefly returns to this subject:

> *That which is above binds that which is below and assimilates it; that which is below is then changed to be like that which is above or is otherwise operated on.*

Reference should also be made to what Agrippa puts on record in his Second Book, chapter XXXII, concerning "The Golden Chain" (of Homer) or "The Ring of Plato."

In connection with the term "sympathy" used toward the end of our main quotation, a striking passage written by the Neoplatonist PLOTINUS (205–270) is worth bringing to the reader's attention. It is as follows: "Since all things in the universe are naturally linked, and the whole is a manifold of forces that attract and repel one another in a variety of ways, and through sympathy (affinity) are united in one life by a single power, it follows that there must be such things as natural magic, theurgy and divination." A similar thought is expressed in chapter LX of the Second Book:

> *Each superior moves the inferior that is immediately below it in rank and order; not only in physical but also in spiritual things.*

METAMORPHOSES OF HUMANS INTO ANIMALS
(Chapter XLI)

Agrippa cites the ancient Roman poet Publius VERGILIUS Maro (70–19 B.C.), whose works were often consulted at random to find sentences that would throw light on the future (*stichomancy*), and who was celebrated in Medieval folklore as something of a wizard. He quotes this reference to the companions of the wanderer ULYSSES (Greek, Odysseus):

Whom Circe, the cruel goddess, transformed by the power of herbs from human shape into animal bodies.

And indeed she changed them into pigs on her island Æaea.[120] As a matter of fact, it has been claimed that "by an intravenous injection of certain glandular secretions of the pig, one can completely change the appearance and color of the body of a person, who will then crawl round the room on all fours—and will be certified as raving mad." One "should not interpret the above verse merely allegorically to the effect that the slaves of fleshly lusts wallow in the mire like dumb brutes, but (so I believe) we can also accept that by giving them animal secretions in intoxicating drinks, this witch physiologically degraded the followers of the king of Ithaca. She had even used her arts on her husband, the king of Sarmatia, and poisoned him to death."[121]

Agrippa has already discussed werewolves. An African equivalent of the European belief in lycanthropy is hyenomania, in which a person is said to change voluntarily into a hyena after the use of certain vegetable poisons.[122] On the other hand, there is a popular belief in China and Japan that animals (foxes) can change themselves into humans ("fox spirits").

---

[120] Homer, *The Odyssey* X, 133 f.
[121] Willy Schrödter, *Vom Hundertsten ins Tausendste* [One Thing and Another], chapter on "Hormones Used in Sorcery," Freiburg/Br., 1940/41, 138.
[122] Schrödter, *Tier-Geheimnisse* [Animal Secrets], 161 f, chapter on "Hyenomania."

MENSTRUAL BLOOD
(Chapter XLII)

By its supervention new wine turns sour; by its contact the vine is irrevocably damaged, and corn withers; seed dies; buds shrivel; fruit falls from the trees; the edge of the razor is blunted; polished ivory loses its shine; iron is rapidly eaten by rust; brass becomes covered in verdigris; dogs that consume it go mad and those who are bitten by these dogs are infected by an incurable poison; the bees die off in the hive and bees flee if it touches their hives; pregnant mares miscarry at its touch; the color of clothes and flowers is spoilt.

Since "everything is food for thought to a genuinely philosophical mind,"[123] we are obliged to study and evaluate these assertions:

1) Effects on the person's own body:
   During the periods waved hair falls out of shape;
   Many times and with many persons, gold rings turn as black as if they were made of base metal.
2) Effects due to contact:
   The Chinese silkworm will not touch mulberry leaves that have been held by a menstruating woman, even if she had spotlessly clean hands.[124]
   Violin strings snap;
   At a spinning-mill in Bayreuth, the adjustment of the static load in spinning synthetic fiber is disturbed by the "field" surrounding the bodies of women during their menses. The yarn does not run or spin smoothly, but ruffles like the hair of many women at this time (Dr. Werner Kaufmann);
   Planting or tending plants during the periods is detrimental to them;

---

[123] Joseph-Ernest Renan, *Mélange d'Histoire et de Voyages* [A Miscellany of Story and Travel], 1878.
[124] Eugen Gregory, *Dreissig Jahre unter Chinesen* [Thirty Years among the Chinese], Stuttgart, 1953.

For the same reason, it is not advisable to pick medicinal herbs during the periods;

Tisanes should not be prepared for invalids, as they would be unwholesome;[125]

Vegetable preserves should not be made as they will spoil;[126]

Preserving jars crack;[127]

Cows should not be milked if the milk is intended for patients;[128]

Lady doctors ought not to operate during their periods (Dr. Busse);

Milk turns sour;

No vinegar, wine or beer should be drawn, or they will go bad or turn sour as the case may be.[129]

3)   Action at a distance:

Breweries must be avoided; otherwise the beer will spoil;[130]

Champagne cellars must be left alone when the wine is fermenting, or else it will spoil;[131]

Sausage factories must be avoided, or the sausages will spoil;

Mushroom farms must be avoided, or the mushrooms will wither (Dr. Kaufmann);

A menstruating woman should not sleep in the same room as a sick person, because the latter's condition can worsen;[132]

Bees leave the hive and readily sting menstruating women.[133]

The notion of "auric infection" is current in Malabar. The view taken there is that a Brahmin becomes unclean if a menstruating woman is less than twelve paces away from him.[134]

---

[125] Hch. Scierbaum, *Heilkräuterbuch,* [The Book of Medicinal Herbs], Pfullingen, n.d., 10.

[126] *Heilkräuterbuch,* p. 10.

[127] *Heilkräuterbuch,* p. 10.

[128] *Heilkräuterbuch,* p. 10.

[129] Adolf Wuttke, *Der dt. Volksaberglaube der Gegenwart* [Popular German Superstitions of Today], Leipzig, 1925; 368 (§ 557).

[130] *Der dt. Volksaberglaube,* 368 (§ 557).

[131] *Der dt. Volksaberglaube,* 426 (§ 668).

[132] *Der dt. Volksaberglaube,* 426 (§ 668).

[133] Andreas Glorez, *Eröffnetes Wunderbuch* [An Open Wonder Book], Regensburg Stadtamhof, 1700, 205.

[134] Prof. G. A. van Rijnberk, *Les Métasciences biologiques* [The Biological Border Sciences], Paris, 1959, 96.

BERSERKERS
(Chapter XLII)

A drink prepared from the brains of a bear and served in the animal's skull is said to produce the fury of a bear, so that a person who has drunk it believes himself to be changed into a bear; he sees everything from a bear's point of view and remains in his madness until the magic of the drink wears off, without suffering any other ill effects.

These statements should be read in conjunction with what was said by Agrippa at the end of his chapter XV: "It is also believed that bear's blood, sucked by mouth from the fresh wound, bestows the immense physical strength that is characteristic of this animal."

Clearly, Agrippa had in mind the so-called "Berserkers" whose mad fighting frenzy is known as "going berserk." The Berserkers originated under Jarl (Earl) HAKON of Trondheim (born 995), and reached their peak under HARALD SCHÖN-HAAR (Harfagr, 860–933), the founder of a united realm of Norway, who was always surrounded by a bodyguard of twelve men who were "high" on some such medication—notoriously so at the decisive battle of Bocksfjord in 872.[135] It was said of them that they were as savage as dogs or wolves and as strong as bulls or bears; they went into battle without armor and were reputed to be proof against fire and steel. Prof. SCHÜBELER in Oedmann ascribes their ecstatic rage to a decoction of fly agaric. But since the latter makes a person cataleptic rather than aggressive—cf., its use in "witches' brews"!—I shall accept Agrippa's explanation until evidence to the contrary turns up.

---

[135] Martin Nink, *Wodan und germanischer Schicksalsglaube* [Woden and Teutonic Fatalism], Jena, 1935, 34.

MAGIC LAMPS
(Chapter XLIX)

Pliny cites Anaxilaus to the effect that, if the poison of mares after copulation is ignited, fantastic heads of horses will be seen, and the same applies to donkeys; midges mixed with wax and set alight produce images of midges, and a snake's skin burned in a lamp gives an appearance of snakes. If, when the vine is in flower one ties a bottle full of oil to it and leaves it there until the grapes are ripe, the images of grapes are said to appear as soon as this oil is burned in a lamp—the same is true of other fruit of the fall. If one mixes centaury with honey and hoopoe blood and prepares a light with it, those present will appear bigger than usual, and if it is lit at night in the open air under a clear sky, the stars will seem to dart about in all directions. The ink of the cuttlefish has the property of making the figures of Moors appear when it is put in a lamp. Similar lights and lamps are mentioned by Hermes, Plato, Chyramides, and later by Albertus in a special treatise.

By ALBERTUS is meant Albertus Magnus, the reputed creator of a garden full of flowers in bloom in the middle of winter (Trithemius), the constructor of androids (automata in human form), whose activities are still commemorated in Paris by the "Place Maubert" (the last word being an abbreviation of the Latin: "Magister Albert"). Popular "Books of Secrets" known as the "Great Albert" and the "Little Albert" have been attributed to him although, in reality, they go back to extremely ancient Chaldean, Egyptian-Arabic, and Greek sources. Even today, in France, "Le Grand Albert" and "Le Petit Albert" are what are meant when one speaks of "grimoires"! Lying on my desk at this very moment is a new edition of these books by H. M. de CAMPIGNY, dated 1937, which actually contains a treatise titled *Wonders of the world and amazing effects* (p. 48 f.), and details several similar lamp recipes.[136]

---

[136] H. M. de Campigny, *Les Secrets admirables du Grand et du Petit Albert* [The Wonderful Secrets of the Great and Little Albert], Paris, 1937/1938 (Garnier frès.).

I should like to see these recipes tested. There must be something in them, because modern conjuring books take the same line. For example, instructions for "making Moors appear" are as follows: "The performer takes a wick made of the pith of a rush and dips it for some time in black ink. This being done, he makes a room completely dark so that not even one ray of light can penetrate it. He now places the prepared wick in a perfectly ordinary lamp and pours oil on it. He lights the lamp and then turns out every other light. A white European lady will change her color to that of a Moorish lady with such a lamp."

The prestidigitator LABERO, whom we have already mentioned, has revealed a "spirit lamp" that actually produces spectral faces: "Some common salt and flowers of sulfur are placed in a porcelain dish and are well stirred in alcohol until dissolved. A lamp wick is inserted in it and lighted. The lamp so made is put in a dark room. An amazingly horrible result will follow: those who are sitting or standing around the lamp will have livid, corpse-like faces; their cheek-bones will look like those of a skull and their eyes will seem quite sunken."[137]

In any case, in yellow sodium light, which consists of virtually one color of the spectrum (wavelength 5890 Å)—that of sodium (Na)—many colors look black, e.g., the red of human lips; and this produces a death-like appearance (Bertelsmann). This light is used in spectroscopy.

FASCINATION
(Chapter L)

Fascination is a binding, which—proceeding from the spirit of the sorcerer—reaches right into the heart of the bewitched. The instrument of fascination is the spirit, i.e., a certain pure, clear, fine vapor created from the purer blood by the heat of the heart, which continually sends rays that are similar to itself through the eyes. These projected rays carry the spiritual vapor in

---

[137] Labéro, 118.

> *them. . . . Thus the open and animated eye, when fixed on someone, shoots its piercing rays, which are the conductors of the spirit, into the eyes of the facing person; and the spirit impelled by the will of the sorcerer strikes the eyes of the subject, enters them, takes possession of his heart and infects that bewitched person with an alien spirit. . . . So the most passionate love is kindled solely by the rays of the eyes; quite often by no more than a quick glance which pierces the whole body like an arrow.*

And when, in the part we have omitted, we read of "steady eye contact," it is obvious that what is being described is some form of hypnosis. Incidentally, it appears from the text that Agrippa adopts the opinion of ARISTOTLE that sight is produced by light emanations from the eyes.

ORGANIC EXTRACTS
(Chapter LI)

It is said that those who dab their eyes three times with the same water in which they wash their feet, will not suffer from any eye disease and will not become bleareyed.

In 1937, a German infirmary released a strange prescription: "Take the water of a bath in which a perfectly healthy person has washed his hands for an hour, and drink 5 to 6 tablespoons of it! It cures heart failure, asthma, pruritis, ulcers, eczema, and diabetes."[138]

Admittedly, there was no mention of "infection with health" (Tenzel, Jäger, Buttenstedt), but of the enrichment of the water with "enzymes"; and instead of the expression "magnetized water" the more scientific sounding term "organic extracts" was used.[139]

---

[138] Anonymous, *Heilkräftiges Badewasser* [Medicinal Bath Water], *Die Koralle,* No. 23, Berlin, July 13, 1937.
[139] Willy Schrödter, *Grenzwissenschaftliche Versuche* [Paranormal Researches], chapter on "Magnetized water."

The shortage of raw materials during the World War led Prof. SCHARZMANN of Germany to revert to "aqua humana" (Latin: human water)—which had fallen into disuse in Europe as a substitute for medicaments that were no longer being manufactured; and the French biologist Marcel CONTIER copied him, reduced the amount of fluid to a fifth by evaporation, pasteurized it, sealed it in ampoules, and injected it with striking success for skin diseases of all kinds.[140]

HUMAN RADIATIONS
(Chapter LV)

Thus a thief hidden in a house creates restlessness, fear, and terror in the owners of the house, even though they do not know or suspect his presence—perhaps not in all of them: for not all, but only a few, people possess a natural instinct of this kind.

Oddly enough, GOETHE (1749–1832) said much the same thing on the evening of October 7, 1827 at the "zum Bären" inn in Jena to Dr. Johann Peter ECKERMANN (1792–1854), later to become a Weimar Court Counsellor: "It is possible or even probable that if—without knowing it—a young girl found herself in a dark room with a man who intended to murder her, she would have an uncanny sense of his presence, and would be overcome by a fear that would drive her out of the room and into the company of her housemates." A contemporary companion-piece comes from the pen of the American writer Prof. Horatio W. DRESSER (1866–1937), professor of philosophy, in his standard work, which has not been surpassed even today: "If one steps into a room in the dark, one can tell from the atmosphere whether or not anyone is present in that room."[141]

Carl Hch. Conr. HUTER was someone who possessed a high degree of the "natural instinct" spoken of by Agrippa, and he based his method of remote sensory diagnosis on it, by devel-

---

[140] Willy Schrödter, *A Rosicrucian Notebook,* York Beach, ME: Samuel Weiser, 1992.
[141] Horatio W. Dresser, *Methoden and Probleme der geistigen Heilbehandlung* [Methods and Problems of Spiritual Healing], Jena, 1902, 40. Translated from the German edition.

oping his talents systematically step by step. "And we must proceed in the same way if we wish to cultivate this ability to the extent that our mental nature allows! First try to detect if anyone is sitting in the room; and then whether male or female; and later on whether the person is big, average-sized, or small, and whether strong, normal, or weak; and finally if certain "targeted" organs of the person reflect anything special to us. Then the distance between the subject and the experimenter is increased. First they occupy adjacent rooms, and afterward, rooms with one, two, etc., intervening rooms."[142]

SENSING LOVED ONES
(Chapter LV)

William of Paris tells of a woman living in his day who had a presentiment of the arrival of a man whom she loved, when he was still two miles away from where she was living.

William of Paris (in French: Guillaume de Paris, also Guillaume d'Auvergne, 1180–1249) was bishop of the Seine metropolis from 1228 and authored "realist" philosophical works. A modern example might be when Helene von DÖNNIGES (1845–1911) was shot dead by her fiancé, Janko von RACOWITZ, in a duel that was fought over her in Geneva. She always felt "a sort of joyful fear" when the popular man approached her unseen, as he did for example in the winter of 1862–1863 in a crowded ballroom in Berlin.[143, 144]

The English novelist of Italian extraction, Marie CORELLI (1864–1924), writes in her account of initiation that exactly the same thing happened to her. This was in the year 1886: "It was growing very late; there were only two more waltzes before the

---

[142] Willy Schrödter, *Grenzwissenschaftliche Versuche* [Paranormal Researches], chapter on "Human Radiations," 145–146.

[143] Enno Nielsen, *Das Große Geheimnis in Neuzeit und Gegenwart* [The Great Secret in Modern and Present Times], Ebenhausen bei Munich, 1923, 181.

[144] H. v. Racowitza, *Von Anderen und mir: Erinnerungen aller Art* [Others and Myself: Mixed Memories], Berlin, 1909–1910; Schrödter, *Präsenzwirkung*, 73.

final cotillon. I was standing near the large open window of the ballroom, conversing with one of my recent partners, when a sudden inexplicable thrill shot through me from head to foot. Instinctively I turned, and saw Cellini approaching."[145] Around 1920, Dr. Gerda WALTHER (born 1897) often used to share a midday meal in Swabian restaurants with the Danish graphologist Jesta BERG, who was then living in Munich. "Jesta BERG was strangely fascinated by the actor Albert STEINRÜCK. . . . Although he almost never wrote to her, she claimed to have intimate knowledge of everything that happened to him."[146] And so, one noon, Jesta BERG leaped to her feet in the middle of a meal because she sensed that, several streets away, her beloved man from Berlin was just getting out of a car!

STORK TRIBUNALS
(Chapter LV)

William of Paris also reports that, in his own lifetime, a stork was convinced by her smell that his mate had been unfaithful. Therefore he convened an assembly of storks and lodged a complaint against the female bird. Upon the latter being unanimously found guilty by the gathered storks, she was pulled about and torn to pieces.

Already before Agrippa, namely in 1355, the Chronicle of Kreuzburg mentions a stork tribunal held for adultery,[147] and stork tribunals convened for the purpose of liquidating unwanted members of the species have been verified right down to the present day![148] Also it is entirely credible that the stork should

---

[145] Marie Corelli, *A Romance of Two Worlds*. Lupton, New York, p. 48; Schrödter: *Präsenzwirkung*, 73.

[146] Dr. Gerda Walther, *Zum anderen Ufer* [To the Other Shore], Remagen, 1960, 255 f.

[147] Paul Quensel, *Thüringische Sagen* [Thuringian Sagas], Jena, 1926, 99.

[148] Schrödter, *Tier-Geheimnisse* [Animal Secrets], 167 f. (A further example appears as No. 498 in the *German Tales of the Brothers Grimm* under the title of "The Faithless Stork.")

rely on his sense of smell to inform him of the adultery of his mate: by having an affair with a third party she was impregnated (or "scented") with the individual Od of the latter. Here are a few instances of the extremely acute sense of smell in animals: wild camels can smell humans up to twelve and a half miles away, which makes them very hard to approach. Wild pigs smell truffles, the parasitic hyphae of which are located on tree roots twelve inches or more below ground. According to Prof. Karl von FRITSCH, a dog will sniff out from a collection of walking-sticks the one that has been touched only briefly by its master's hand, even when it has been rubbed with oil of cloves. Now oil of cloves has such a penetrating scent that even a human with an average sense of smell, having 80 million olfactory cells, can detect 0.000,000,04 in 1 cc of air!

ODIC FLAMES
(Chapter LVI)

When the wife of Tarquinius Priscus saw a flame licking the head of Servius Tullius, she predicted that he would receive the kingdom. Similarly, after the sack of Troy, when Aeneas was debating with his father Anchises about the advisability of flight, a flame appeared on the crown of the head of Ascanius without harming him, and this event foretelling that Ascanius would have the kingdom, persuaded them to emigrate.

In chapter LXIII we read:

What can be done by violent anger joined with daring courage may be seen in Alexander the Great who, when in India, radiated fire and light in the midst of the fray. Also we read of the father of Theoderich that he emitted fiery sparks from his whole body, and that these sparks even made a noise as they leapt from various sides. The same thing happens to animals, as is related of a horse owned by Tiberius that it spat flames.

In chapter XLIII of the Third Book our author returns to this theme again:

> *History tells of Alexander the Great, who displayed such courage when in extreme danger in India, that the Barbarians imagined he was radiating light.*[149] *What is more, the father of Theoderich was said to have showered sparks from all over his body. A certain sage related the same thing of himself, and in his case the phenomenon was so powerful that the sparks leapt from him audibly. Now this property of the soul may be observed not only in humans but also in animals; as for example in a horse belonging to Tiberius which is alleged to have spat flames.*

We know of Buddhist paintings in which personages are represented who have flames of fire rising from their breasts and sex organs.[150] Whatever else may be said of them, these are the so-called "Odic Flames," identified mainly in humans by the scientist and industrialist Baron von REICHENBACH (1788–1869), the "Wizard of Kobenzl" (near Vienna) in the middle of the last century, concerning which he wrote nine books, some of which are bulky tomes.

"Anyone who reads in his writings how he performed ca. 12,000 tests of the most varied kinds on about 150 persons of all stations in life and under the most stringent conditions, will acknowledge—once he or she grasps the magnitude of his achievement—that the existence of Od is as well-established as

---

[149] Alexandra David-Neel, *Magic and Mystery in Tibet*, Dover, New York, 1971; Dr. Heinrich Biek, *Kann Hypnose heilen?* [Can Hypnosis Cure?], Neustadt (Weinstraße), 1957, 35–36; (Dr. Emil Franzel) Boeheim, Carl von, *Unter dem Hradschin* [Among the Hradshin], Augsburg, 1962, 401; An article on the halo of sainthood in *Die Andere Welt*, No. 3, Freiburg, March, No. 4 April, 1963, 184 f; 272 f.

[150] So-called "superhuman strength" is brought into play by life-threatening situations, by fires, and by mad fits of rage, etc. Aikido, a Far-Eastern method of self-defense, seeks to produce this condition artificially (Johns). The alphabet mystic, J. B. Kerning (Joh. Bapt. Krebs, 1774–1851) taught in his *Key to the Spiritual World* (Lorch/Wttbg.) what he termed the "arousal of the inner Samson power" (Schrödter, *Paranormal Researches*, 28).

almost anything can be," says one modern naturopath.[151] The world grasped the hand of the learned industrialist with his paraffin, creosote, eupions, picamar, and capnomor, but rebuffed him over Od, which it regarded as nonexistent.

To this may be attributed the fact that REICHENBACH'S Od is constantly being rediscovered and overlaid with new names such as the "N-rays" (for "Nancy"-rays) of the physicist René-Prosper BLONDLOT (1849–1930), professor at the University of Nancy. His university colleague, the physician, physiologist, and neurologist, Professor Pierre Marie Augustin CHARPENTIER (1852–1916) assisted him in the development of his research.[152]

The so-called "aureole" and its maximum expression "transfiguration," are connected with the phenomenon of odic flames. Agrippa (III; 43) gives us an example of this:

Socrates is said to have been so transfigured
that he outshone the brightness of the sun.

There is no need for me to discuss the reality of the aureole and of transfiguration here, as I have done so elsewhere.[153] I shall merely mention, regarding the story of the flame that sprang from the top of the head of Ascanius, that mental excitement can make the hair stand on end at this place.

After the above was written, I found in Dr. EDKIN'S *Religions of China* that the Buddhist "Wu–Wei" sect teaches how to induce intense excitement by the imagination; if this is done when one is in a state of repose, "sparks are emitted from the eyes of the meditator."

---

[151] Dr. Gustav Riedlin, *Grundursachen der Krankheiten und wahre Heilmittel* [Fundamental Causes of Diseases and True Remedies], Lorch/W., 1922, 176.
[152] Willy Schrödter, *Präsenzwirkung* [On the Nature of Healing Through Contact], Ulm/Donau, 1960, 39.
[153] Schrödter, *Präsenzwirkung*, 126 f.

STRANGE RAINS
(Chapter LVI)

*Thus we read in Pliny that during the consulate of M.
Antilius and C. Portius it is said to have rained milk
and blood, indicating that in the following year a severe plague would visit Rome. Likewise it rained
spongy iron in Lucania one year before M. Crassus
was killed in Parthia, and all the Lucanian soldiers, of
whom there were a great number in the army, perished
with him. In the same way, during the consulate of L.
Paulsus and C. Marcellus, it rained wool near the
Corisanum citadel, where T. Annius Milo was slain a
year later. When describing the Macedonian war, Livy
says: in the year Hannibal died, it rained blood for two
days; and in his account of the second Punic war he
says that it was reported that, in the period when Hannibal was laying Italy waste, water mingled with blood
fell from the sky in the form of rain.*

Agrippa takes it for granted that "all great misfortunes are her-
alded by miraculous portents and remarkable events." In other
words he regards the extraordinary natural phenomena just described as omens!

It can easily be ascertained that unusual rains of this sort
are well attested right up to modern times, and are caused by
wind-made admixtures of such things as desert sand and pollen,
dust, etc. Unfortunately, my interesting collection of recent cases
in point has been lost, but I am able to produce some from the 16th
through the 18th centuries with the help of BUCHNER'S well-
known sidelights on social history abstracted from old German
newspapers and magazines.[154] Thus it was reported from Vienna
on June 25, 1620 that for eight consecutive days the water in the
city moat "had looked as if it had been changed into blood."

Also, according to an announcement in the Holsteinischen
for January 1, 1692, it rained blood smelling of rotten strawberries

---

[154] Eberhard Buchner, *Medien, Hexen und Geisterseher* [Mediums, Witches, and Spiritists],
Munich, 1926, Articles 21, 27, 34, 35, 40, 41, 42, 43; p. 35 f.

not far from Lübeck. Here we have an indirect hint of the vegetable nature of the coloring.

Apparently, if we are to believe a news item dated August 4, 1694, a tornado whirled a quantity of millet into the sky from somewhere or other and—much to the joy of the poor inhabitants—deposited it on Breslau. Particularly interesting, because it is so informative, is a report from Bordeaux dated April 25, 1761. It appeared in the *Haude-Spenersche Zeitung* [newspaper] No. 59 and we quote it below in full:

> The wind being in the southwest on the first of the month in this place, a light rain fell between 11 and 12 o'clock with a yellow powder-like saffron, but somewhat brighter in color. This powder covered the whole town to a depth of 2 lines [approximately 1/5 inch]. The townsfolk, who had never seen anything like it, were alarmed. Everyone voiced an opinion, and many saw it as a sign of the end of the world. However, our natural philosophers and other level-headed citizens collected samples of the powder and quickly found that this phenomenon was far from being a miraculous sign. It was nothing more than pollen from the flowers of the fir trees growing in the countryside south of Bordeaux. Without doubt, a whirlwind from the southwest had picked up a huge quantity of it and, after carrying it here, had spread it over the entire town. More fell on the 21st and was found to have the same character as before.

While writing this, I have come across a recent example: "Yesterday 'diamond-dust' fell on Freising (Bavaria) out of a cloudless sky. The needles looked like tiny feathers and consisted of a number of crystals frozen togther. 'Diamond-dust' is formed only when the humidity of the air is high and the weather is icy cold."[155]

---

[155] "Seltsame Naturphänomeme" [Rare Natural Phenomena] in the *Westfälische Rundschau*, Dortmund 21./22. 1, 1961.

LEAD POURING
(Chapter LVII)

Among these (i.e., the four elementary arts of divina-
tion, geomancy, hydromancy, aeromancy, and pyro-
mancy) can be reckoned the art of pouring molten lead
or wax into water in order to obtain clear images of the
thing one wants to know.

Lead-pouring on New Year's Eve is still in vogue even today. On the other hand, wax-pouring has gone out of fashion. A priest who was aware of his approaching death poured a four-inch-high *pietà* [sculpture of the Virgin Mary holding the dead body of Christ] very like the one standing in his church.[156]

ADSPIRATION AND INSUFFLATION
(Chapter LVIII)

. . . just as a weasel is brought back to life by the breath
and voice of its mother, or as a lioness reanimates her
dead cubs by breathing on them.

It is not quite clear from the text whether our author has in mind breathing on for which the technical term "adspiration" has been coined, or is thinking of breathing into, known as "insufflation." Therefore we shall comment on both types of magnetizing, which are pretty much neglected today.

And first breathing on, or adspiration: The court physician and Hofrat of Saxony, Prof. Carl Gustav CARUS (1789–1869) made the striking statement in 1857 that "the warm breath of a healthy person affects us quite differently from a mechanically produced steam-heated stream of air having exactly the same temperature and humidity."[157] In 1815, in his classic book

---

[156] Peter Fischer, "Wunderbarer Bleiguß am Silvesterabend" [Amazing Lead Pouring on New Year's Eve] in *Die Andere Welt,* Part 12, Freiburg I. B., December, 1965, 1100 f.
[157] Carus, 105.

on magnetism,[158] an old magnetist with a great reputation, professor of surgery at the Royal Military Academy of Medicine and Surgery in Berlin, Dr. Carl Alexander Ferdinand KLUGE (1782–1844) had much to say about the "breathing on" technique and its results.[159] Also the late, very well-known vital-energy healer, the engineer Rudolf THETTER (1882–1957) of Vienna, recommended aspiration of the pit of the stomach for fainting fits: "The unconscious person will soon regain consciousness and will wake up with extra energy,[160] as I myself have found out."

Recently, French magnetizers have obtained lasting results in desperate cases of infectious fevers running a rapid course (typhoid and puerperal fevers, bronchitis, pneumonia, and meningitis) through what Dr. Henri DURVILLE (Paris) calls "La Transfusionvitale" ["Transfusion of vitality"]: which consists of breathing for several hours together on the place to be influenced, and especially on the pit of the patient's stomach.[161] And now to take a look at the less hygienic but certainly more effective insufflation! The Old Testament [The Tenakh] describes how the prophet ELISHA (ca. 850 B.C.) raised from the dead his Shunamite hostess's son (who may have succumbed to influenza?).

> And he went up, and lay upon the child, and put his mouth upon his mouth, and his eyes upon his eyes, and his hands upon his hands: and he stretched himself upon the child; and the flesh of the child waxed warm. Then he returned, and walked in the house to and fro [Hebrew: once hither, and once thither]; and went up, and stretched himself upon him; and the child sneezed seven times, and the child opened his eyes.[162]

The Hebrew parchment MS of a magician's Testament of 1387 recommends Elisha's method of "measuring oneself on the patient"

---

[158] Kluge, 321–322.
[159] Schrödter, *Grenzwissenschaftliche Versuche* [Paranormal Research], 92–93 "Healing Magnetism."
[160] Rudolf Thetter, *Magnetismus-das Urheilmittel* [Magnetism—the Original Form of Cure], Vienna, 1951, 226.
[161] Henri Durville, *La Transfusion vitale* [The Transfusion of Vitality], Paris, 1923; A. Hartmann, *Die Lebenskraftübertragung* [The Transmission of Vitality], in "Der Lebenskraftheiler"; Parts 1 & 2, Wiesbaden 1932.
[162] II Kings, 4: 34–35 [KJV with marginal note. Tr.].

and of "insufflation" in order to "arouse someone who is in a coma or dead."[163]

This method was "accidentally" discovered by one of the chosen "Knights of the Golden Stone"—or ROSICRUCIANS. He "embraced" his dead sweetheart "clasped her in his arms, felt her heart, wished to 'kiss her enough' (which almost amounts to insufflation), and was overjoyed to discover that her heart took up more and more of his heat, so that she actually still lived." He brought his bride completely back to life, by "warming her body with a rich herbal lotion."[164]

In case anyone should run away with the idea that this episode is pure fiction, I have given examples from real life in one of my other books.[165] The court physician Pierre BOREL (1620-1689) relates how a servant revived his dead master by this means.[166] The "Vossische Zeitung" (Berlin, 1773; No. 12) reports:

At Montiers, near Amiens in France, a 4-year-old child recently fell into the river Bresse and was not pulled out until an hour later. He was put to bed and covered with sheets and blankets. After two more hours an expert arrived, laid himself on the child's body, and blew strongly into the mouth of the child while shutting the latter's nose. The child was restored to life.[167]

---

[163] *Des Juden Abraham von Worms Buch der wahren Praktik in der uralten göttlichen Magie usw.* [The Book of the Jew Abraham of Worms Concerning the Age-Old Divine Magic, etc.], Cologne, 1725, 46. Nevertheless, although the Bible says that Elisha laid his mouth on the child's mouth (as he also laid his eyes on his eyes and his hands on his hands), it does not describe him specifically giving the child mouth-to-mouth resuscitation. We *are* told, however, that after shutting the door on himself and the dead child Elisha "prayed unto the Lord" (v. 33). It seems fairly obvious that he was not giving the "kiss of life" but was following some other procedure, involving mouth, eyes and hands, which, if we knew the reason for it, might prove to be deeply interesting. Tr. note.]

[164] *Chymische Hochzeit Christiani Rosencreutz* A.D. 1459 (IIIter Tag) [*The Chymical Wedding of Christian Rosenkreutz* (The Third Day)]. Straßburg, 1616. English translation by E. Foxcroft, London 1690 (reprinted in: *A Christian Rosenkreutz Anthology,* Spiritual Science Library, New York, 1968, 1981).

[165] Schrödter, *A Rosicrucian Notebook,* Samuel Weiser, York Beach, ME, 1992.

[166] Petrus Borellus, *Historiarum et observationum, medico-physicarum centuriae IV, in quibus non sola multa utilia, sed et rara, stupenda ac inaudita continentur* [Four Sets of One Hundred of Medico-Physical Accounts and Observations, Containing not only Much Useful Matter but Much that is Rare, Amazing, and Out of the Ordinary], Paris, 1657, Cent. III; Obs. 58.

[167] Eberhard Buchner, *Ärzte und Kurpfuscher* [Doctors and Empirics], Munich 1922; 263; No. 327.

But often insufflation is performed at the other end; just as inhalation narcosis corresponds to rectal narcosis. Thus according to the "Vossische Zeitung" (Berlin, 1758; No. 56), it was reported from Haarlem [in The Netherlands] on April 26 concerning a small boy who had drowned an hour previously that "finally a lime-burner blew through a tobacco pipe into the backside of the victim of the accident, and within two minutes some signs of movement appeared in the latter's body; and after the treatment had been continued for an hour the child regained consciousness."[168] This method was most emphatically recommended by the celebrated natural philosopher René Antoine Ferchault de REAUMUR (1683–1757) in a work published in 1740. What is more, a contemporary mesmerist has faith in it and still employs the method in suitable cases.

Professor Oskar KORSCHELT (1841–1940) declared in 1891: "Human healing power is conveyed more strongly by the breath than it is by the hand. A clean cloth is spread over the afflicted part, and the open mouth is pressed over it and breathes on it without interruption. The effect is extraordinarily stimulating to the whole organism of the patient. When a relay of healthy individuals breathed for some hours on the pit of the stomach of a dying person, the latter was kept alive; in fact, the same procedure has even been successful in revivifying the dead."[169] In 1947, the dental surgeon, Harry B. WRIGHT, is standing with the well known female witch-doctor of Bapende (Zaire [at that time the Belgian Congo]) in front of a dying girl about 8 years old. With his finger on her wrist, he can no longer feel her pulse, and he can hear no heart beats through the stethoscope. "She is dead. But LUSUNGU shakes her head. She crouched beside the girl and began to breathe into her mouth. I shall never fathom how she knew that there was still a spark of life in the child when my medical instruments said differently. Anyway, the girl's lips soon began to move, and I could feel a pulse. . . ." She began to speak.[170]

The following are some quite recent cases of the effect of insufflation *in extremis*: In 1957, Mrs. Lorna GRIFFIS of Redfern near Sidney (Australia) restored to life through insufflation the

---

[168] Buchner, 257 f.; No. 317.
[169] Korschelt, 69.
[170] Harry B. Wright, *Zauberer und Medizinmänner* [Sorcerers and Medicine-Men], Zürich, 1958, 93 f.

apparently dead premature baby of her neighbor Mrs. Phil. ROBERTSON.[171] Also in 1957 in England, during a game played in Rainham (Essex) against Rainham Town, the joiner and amateur footballer of Basildon Football Club, Ronald WYNN, was hit in the stomach by a ball kicked from a distance of four feet. He sank to the ground and his breathing and heartbeats stopped. The trainer of the Rainham team, Bill TITHERINGTON (remembering what he had seen in a film) blew into his mouth, and after six minutes his efforts were successful: WYNN started breathing again and stood up.[172]

Finally, in 1961, "Mrs. Peggy PROUDLOCK of Bedlington (England) gave birth to quaduplets. One of these died at birth, and then the weakest of the three remaining children suddenly stopped breathing. The frightened mother used an age-old method to save the baby; she placed her mouth on that of the child and breathed air into its lungs. The doctor who had been called in assured the mother that by doing what she did she had saved her child." I have in front of me as I write a picture of the happy mother with her husband and children.[173] An English esotericist, with whom I corresponded on this subject at the end of 1961, wrote to me: "Insufflation has recently been used here quite often as a method of resuscitation. The newspapers are full of it. Over here it is known as 'the kiss of life.'"

All these successes have led to the official recommendation that, in heart attacks, instead of direct heart massage after the chest has been surgically opened, pressure should be applied to the chest while mouth-to-mouth resuscitation is being used. "The wrist of the right hand is laid on the breast-bone [sternum] immediately over the heart, the left hand is placed on top of it and is thrust downward briefly and strongly to a depth of about an inch. This forces the blood out of the heart into the main arteries. The chest is then released, so that it can expand and allow blood to flow back into the heart from the vena cava. Then there is another thrust and another release at the rate of seventy times per minute, until regular breathing is restored. This form of heart massage should be supported if possible by mouth-to-mouth resuscitation, when a second helper is available to give it and force oxygen into

---

[171] "Neue Illustrierte Wochenschau" (No. 40, October 6), Vienna, 1957, 3.
[172] "Neue Illustrierte Wochenschau" (No. 46, November 17), Vienna, 1957, 3.
[173] "Neue Illustrierte Wochenschau" (No. 41, October 8), Vienna, 1961, 18.

the inactive lungs. This method was developed by the electrical engineer Dr. KOUWENHOVEN in collaboration with medical staff at the hospital of the Johns Hopkins University in Baltimore (USA) after two years of tests on dogs."[174]

And, speaking of animals: "Rita, a female chimpanzee in Dresden Zoo, made desperate attempts to resuscitate her premature baby, which had died soon after birth. *Die Union* described how the mother opened the baby's mouth with her paws, pulled out its tongue with her lips as far as she could, and then blew her breath down the throat of the little one," although, of course, the latter was beyond help.[175]

In the summer of 1965, on a flight from Stockholm to Majorca, Señora de Alcoveery Sureda, the wife of the Spanish ambassador to Sweden, became unconscious. Stewardess Eva Magnussen (born in 1941) tried to revive the lady—who was now breathing hard—with ice-bags and oxygen, but to no avail. So then, for two hours, she gave mouth-to-mouth resuscitation. By touch-down in Palma the paitient had been saved! And the stewardess was completely done in.[176]

PRANIC NOURISHMENT
(Chapter LVIII)

Around that time (i.e., in the days of Giovanni Boccaccio, 1313–1375) there was a woman in North Germany who took no food until she was 13 years old; which would seem incredible if an amazing instance of the same sort had not presented itself in our own times. It is a well-known fact that Brother Nikolaus von der Flue, a Helvetian, lived in the wilderness for over twenty years until his death without taking any food.

In fact, for twenty years, Niklas LÖWENBRUGGER (1417–1487) took nothing more than a communion wafer each evening,

---

[174] "Das ist der Griff, der Ihr Leben retten kann" [This is the Hold that Can Save Your Life] in *Bild-Zeitung* of June 7, Frankfurt/M., 1961, 6.

[175] "Der Schmerz einer Tiermutter" [The Grief of an Animal Mother] in *Schweizer Ill. Ztg.* (No. 7, February 13), Zofingen, 1961, 25.

[176] "Zwei-Stunden-Kuß rettete Frau das Leben" [Two-Hour Kiss Saved a Woman's Life], in *Bild-Zeitung*, No. 152, July 5, 1965.

which one cannot regard as nourishment in the ordinary sense! And he is certainly not the only saint who did not need coarse food. Lack of dependence on food was cultivated through special training by Indian[177] and Chinese[178] yogis. Through the technique of "Kryayoga" the female yogi Giri BALA, of Nawaggan (Ganges) (born in 1868) managed to survive without food and drink from her twelfth year onwards.[179]

However one can arrive at this peculiar condition without training. Thus YANG MEI of Chongging (born in 1927) has taken nothing but water since 1939 after losing the desire for food through eating a bulbous fruit (perhaps some kind of toadstool is meant?).[180] As a sequel to an illness, Marie FURTNER of Frasdorf (Upper Bavaria) (1823–1884) acquired an aversion from solid food when she was 12 years old and, from that time onward until shortly before her death, she nourished herself on 1½ liters [a little over 2½ pints] of spring water per day; except for a few weeks in spring, when she also took freshly tapped birch sap.[181] Therese NEUMANN of Konnersreuth (1898–1962) said when asked that "her life without food might have arisen from a year-long illness."[182] Similarly, Therese FREUTMIEDL of Hart a. d. Alz bei Mühldorf (Southeast Bavaria) (1904–1961) partook only of pure water and the consecrated host subsequent to an illness in 1950, because she simply felt no hunger pangs.[183]

---

[177] A.M. Oppermann, *Yoga-Aphorismen des Patanjali* [The Yoga Aphorisms of Patanjali], Leipzig, 1925, 69 (III; 30) ["Concentrate on the hollow of the throat; go beyond hunger and thirst," *Aphorisms of Yôga* by Bhagwân Shree Patanjali, translated by Shree Purohit Swâmi, Faber & Faber, London, 1973, 68].

[178] Ed. Erkes, "Die taoistische Meditation u. ihre Bedeutung f. d. chin. Geistesleben" [Taoist Meditation and its Significance in Chinese Spiritual Life] in *Psyche*, Part 3, Heidelberg, 1949, 377.

[179] Paramahamsa Yogananda, *The Autobiography of a Yogi*, Self-Realization, Los Angeles, 1973, and many other editions.

[180] G.E. Ledoux, "Seit neun Jahren ohne jegliche Nahrung" [Nine Years without any Form of Food] in *Cigognes*, No. 32, Strasbourg, Aug. 8, 1948. Anonymous, "Okkultes a. d. Fernen Osten" [Occult Matters in the Far East] in *Das neue Licht*, Part 3, Wien-Purkersdorf, 1949, 51 f.

[181] K. E. v. Schafhäutel, *Die Wassertrinkerin Jungfr. Marie Furtner aus Frasdorf in Oberbayern, etc.* [The Water-Drinking Girl Marie Furtner of Frasdorf in Upper Bavaria, etc.] (new impression), Dresden, 1937.

[182] Erkes, "Tie Taoistische Meditation . . .," 377–387.

[183] Frz. V. Schöffel, "Eine 'Wassertrinkerin' der Gegenwart" [A Present-Day Woman who Lives on Nothing but Water] in *Das neue Licht*, Parts 2-3, Wien-Purkersdorf, Feb./ Mar. 1956, 42–43; Anonymous, "Seit sechs Jahren lebt sie nur von Wasser" [She has Lived on Nothing but Water for Six Years] in *Neue Ill. Wochenschau*, No. 27, July 1, 1956, 3; Josef Bader, "Zehn Jahre lang nur Wasser als Nahrung" [Water the Only Nourishment for Ten Years] in *Neue Württ. Zeitung*, Stuttgart, July 17, 1961.

What can we make of all this? Science has labeled such cases as *nutritio spiritualis* (Latin: spiritual nourishment) or as *inedia* (Latin: not eating). When his disciples urged Jesus to eat something, he replied: "My meat is to do the will of him that sent me, and to finish his work."[184] Clearly, God does not allow the bearers of His revelation to starve on the earthly plane when they are so absorbed in His service that they forget their human need for sustenance—as Sadhu SUNDAR SINGH (1889–1932) testified concerning himself.

Nevertheless, in my opinion, one need not look as far afield as this; certainly not in those who have no saintly vocation. What happens is that coarse-grained nourishment is replaced by subtle nourishment. The Taoist writings refer to "air-eating," the Indian adepts maintain that a subtle air or "super-air" they call *prana* is contained in the atmospheric air, and they have developed a special breathing technique known as *pranayama* for its intake.

In about 1927, Chaplain Kurt KRAUS noticed how a religious devotee whose body was impressed with the stigmata, and for a long time had eaten hardly anything, would stretch out her hands during her ecstasies, in order to take from the air a whey-like substance to put in her mouth. This could well be condensed prana being supplied to the etheric body.[185] Just as the Berlin physiologist Prof. Otto Heinrich WARBURG (born in 1883), Nobel prize-winner in 1931, announced in 1929 that air contains a ferment similar to haemin which probably is as important as the vitamins in ordinary feeding,[186] so in 1952 the Scottish biochemist Prof. Alexander Robertus TODD (born in 1907) of the University of Cambridge, Nobel prize-winner in 1957, demonstrated that we actually take in vitamins (coenzymes) with the air we breathe and that only by absorbing a sufficient supply of them can life be maintained. A special form of breathing or etherealization would certainly be involved here[187] which so tightens up the network of our "cellular sieve" that the

---

[184] St. John IV: 31–34.
[185] K. Haenig, "Zur Nahrungsenthaltung kath. Heiliger" [The Abstention from Food of Catholic Saints] in *Ztrbl. f. Okk.,* Leipzig, March, 1928, 428–429.
[186] Anonymous, "Prana wiss. bestätigt (Vitamine i. d. Luft)" [Scientific Confirmation of Prana (Vitamins in the Air)], in *Ztrbl. f. Okk.,* Leipzig, 1929, 332.
[187] Willy Schrödter, *Grenzw. Versuche* [Paranormal Researches], chapter on "Pranic nourishment," 213–215.

finer forces that usually flow through it are retained. In any case, it has been known since 1930 that we can drink through the skin. Thus university lecturer Dr. E. URBACH reported that a female patient in his skin clinic absorbed 13,287 g and secreted 16,040 g in six days ("Med Klinik"; 1933; Part 55).

In conclusion we need only refer to analogous cases in the vegetable kingdom: Florida moss (*Tillandsia usneoides*), Aloes (*Aloe vulg. La.*) and Rose of Jericho (*Anastatica hierochuntica*).[188]

MEDIUMISTIC ABILITIES
(Chapter LX)

The power of the melancholic disposition is said to be so great that heavenly spirits are sometimes attracted into the human body by it . . . and this is believed to happen in three different ways: by imagination, understanding, and reason. . . . If the soul is driven by the melancholy humor, the restraints of the body and its members being shaken off and everything passing into the imagination, it immediately becomes the dwelling place of demons of the lower rank, which often confer on it a wonderful facility in arts of every kind. Thus we see the most uneducated person suddenly becoming a splendid painter or architect or a master in some other art. . . . But if the soul is converted quite into understanding, it becomes the dwelling place of middle-ranking entities and obtains knowledge and understanding of natural and human things. And so the individual speedily becomes an eminent philosopher, physician or public speaker. . . . Lastly, if the soul completely elevates itself to pure reason,[189] it becomes the dwelling place of higher spirits and learns divine secrets from them.

---

[188] Willy Schrödter, *Pflanzen-Geheimnisse* [Plant Secrets], chapter on "Plants and Pranic Nourishment," 85–86.

[189] In the text lying before me the (German) translation is "to the understanding," while the translation in another source has "to divine thoughts." I have chosen the term "pure reason," on the one hand because it is in accordance with AGRIPPA'S own threefold division and, on the other hand, because pure reason is compatible with a comprehension of the moral and the divine.

The existence of trance painters, for example, "is testified by the whole of Antiquity" (so we read in the dotted omission of the second sentence), and as far as the present day is concerned, mention need be made only of the widely known—at least in Germany—Nuremberg "picture-writer" Wilhelm NÜSSLEIN (see the chapter on mummifying caves). Representative of the "spiritual healers" are Gustav Adolf Egmont Roderich MÜLLER-CZERNY (1862–1922), the "miracle doctor of Bad Homburg"[190] and the British spiritual healer Harry ED-WARDS;[191] and a "master of other arts" is the "trance writer" Robert KRAFT.[192]

SHARED SENSATIONS
(Chapter LXIII)

As we know, the bond of love between lovers is often so strong that what one endures is also suffered by the other.

"Living in France there is a marquis who is an occultist. With a naturally delicate psychological make-up, having had a refined upbringing, and being protected by wealth from the rough edges of life, yet purified by suffering and resignation, he made contact with the higher forms of existence called astral lives by Theosophists. His sensitivity was in fact so highly developed that he became a receiver and was able to enter into a state of rapport with friends living far away."[193] The Marquis Joseph Alexandre St. Yves d'ALVEYDRE (1842–1909), the person in question, married the Comtesse de KELLER. She was, as it happened, a niece of Mme.

---

[190] Willy Schrödter, *Präsenzwirkung*, 167.
[191] Harry Edwards, "Spirit Healing."
[192] Robert Kraft, *Die Augen der Sphinx: Eine kurze Lebensbeschreibung von ihm selbst verfaßt* [The Eyes of the Sphinx: An Autobiographical Sketch], Dresden-Niedersetzlitz, n.d.; Willy Schrödter, *Grenzwiss. Versuche* [Paranormal Researches], 107.
[193] August Strindberg, *Ein neues Blaubuch* [A New Blue Book], chapter on "Mighty Love," Munich, 1920, 807. This and the following quotes are from Marie de Rabutin-Chantal, Marquise de Sévigné (1626–1696) who made the following classic remark to her daughter Francoise-Marguerite ("the prettiest girl in France"), later the Countess Grignan (1646–1705), who was painfully racked by a chronic cough: "My child, I have pains in your chest!"

Evelyn de BALZAC (1801–1882), the widowed Countess HANS-KA, née RZEWUSKA, wife of the novelist Honoré de BALZAC (1799–1850). "These spouses are so united that one would think that each is born within the other." Mesmerism uses the technical term *neurogamy* (Greek for "nerve marriage") for this condition. "When, on a visit to relatives, she was so alarmed by shying horses that her heart started thumping, he felt it in his own chest, and his heart stopped for a moment when she fainted. On the other hand, once when he pricked himself with a needle she felt it."

Early one morning in 1880, while out sailing, the English landscape painter Arthur SEVERN was badly cut on the upper lip by the tiller as it swung in a sudden gust of wind; and his wife, who had stayed at home, awoke at about 7 o'clock feeling that she had received a severe blow on the mouth, and there was blood over her upper lip. The married couple certified this incident in letters dated October 27, 1883, mailed from their Brantwood estate near Coniston (Lancashire) to Prof. RUSKIN, and he recorded it in the prestigious "Proceedings" of the newly-formed Society for Psychical Research, in London, which had commenced publication in 1882.[194]

In 1956 a Mr. G. of W. wrote to me: "A lady, with whom I have close ties of affection, suffered from a severe crying fit on November 16, 1953. At the same time my chest was gripped by a sense of constriction that led to suppressed sobbing. The distance between us was nine miles. A community of feeling of this sort between two individuals (French: *bipersonalité;* Latin: *dipsychicum*), confirms a saying of Marcus Portius CATO, the elder, (234–149 B.C.): 'The soul of a lover lives in another body.'"[195] Apart from lovers, it is blood-relatives who experience shared sensations most often, as may be seen in our next example: "In 1944, when walking in the park in Mährisch-Ostrau, the very lively Austrian girl Maria HAIDER suddenly fainted and was later informed that on the same day (August 12) and at the same hour, her elder brother had received a fatal bullet wound in the chest.[196] However, it is in identical twins that neurogamy occurs

---

[194] Albert de Rochas, *Ausscheidung des Empfindungsvermögens* [The Secretion of Sensitivity], Leipzig, 1909, 393 f.

[195] Willy Schrödter, *Präsenzwirkung*, 99.

[196] Heading from "Das Kaleidoskop" in *Neue Ill. Wochenschau*, No. 27, Vienna, August 8, 1958, 27.

most frequently and to the greatest extent—in both senses of the word, i.e., both to the extent of the phenomena and to the extent of the distance covered.[197]

REFLEXES
(Chapter LXIV)

Quite often the passions of the soul act on the body by way of imitation . . . when a vivid imagination comes into play as, for example . . . when we see someone eating sour things or even think about it. Whoever sees anyone else yawning, yawns too, and many persons get an acid taste in the mouth when they hear vinegar mentioned. Looking at something filthy alters the taste and causes nausea. Many faint at the sight of human blood. Some taste a bitter saliva in their mouths if anyone is served a bitter food in front of their eyes. CARUS (who has been mentioned already in the section on "Taste Perversions") has two examples to offer: "If anyone is given a vivid description of a lemon being cut in half, or if one is actually cut in half in front of a person, the muscle fibers of the salivary ducts immediately contract under the influence of the gray nerve fibers, and spittle is felt accumulating in the mouth."[198] A practical joker who was sitting in the front row at a brass band concert put on a display of sinking his teeth into a juicy lemon. The musicians' mouths watered[199] and they were unable to go on playing. This is the so-called "ideosecretory phenomenon."[200]

"If, say, we think of someone accidentally sticking a penknife in the middle of his eye, then without such a horrible thing happening the very idea will immediately and unavoidably give

---

[197] Willy Schrödter, *Präsenzwirkung*, 93 f; and "Schicksals-Gleichheit bei E-Zwillingen" [Similar Fates in Identical Twins] in *Die Andere Welt*, Freiburg, 1966, March, No. 3, 66 f; April, No. 4, 66 f.

[198] Carus, 169 f.

[199] Over the years, the color yellow has become almost synonymous with lemons: little children who are given raspberry-flavored candies colored yellow start salivating before they put them in their mouths, because they are mistakenly expecting citric acid to be present! (Joh. Uhlmann) But adults react in the same way: in a test run in New York in 1960, 45 housewives were offered yellow ices flavored with raspberry, and 42 of them said how much they liked the lemon taste!

[200] Willy Schrödter, *Grenzw. Vers.* [Paranormal Researches], chapter on "Reflexes," 233 f.

us an uncomfortable feeling in our own eye. This lends feasibili-
ty to the alleged influence of a pregnant woman's imagination
on the fetus."[201] It is the so-called "maternal impressions" of
pregnancy. "When someone close to us of whom we are fond
(thus not someone we care nothing about) gives us a vivid description of some bad pain he or she has been suffering, icy fingers seem to run down our back and it makes our flesh creep like
the rider over Lake Constance"![202]

SEX CHANGE
(Chapter LXIV)

*Pliny himself produces many examples of women who
were changed into men, and Pontanus testifies that the
same thing happened in his own lifetime to a woman of
Cajeta and to a certain Emilia, who after being married
for some years, were turned into men.*

A modern parallel is to be found in the autobiography of Roberta
COWELL: "I was a man," the most incredible true story ever
written, in which an English racing driver, bomber pilot, and father of two, became a successful woman. This unlikely female
described her unique and poignant fate in a matter-of-fact way
and grabbed the world headlines. Further cases, supported by il-
lustrations, have been written up in the German weeklies.[203] The
PONTANUS (Giovano Pontano, 1426–1503) cited above was an
Italian statesman, poet, and historian and one of the best Latin
authors of the 15th century.

---

[201] Carus, 131; Willy Schrödter, "Über das Versehen Schwangerer" [Maternal Impres-
sions] in *Die Andere Welt*, No. 6, Freiburg, June, 1966, 507 f.

[202] Schrödter, *Grenzw. Vers.* [Paranormal Researches], 234. Schrödter assumes that any
German reader would know what he is talking about here, but it is not clear to English
readers. The reference is to a narrative poem of 62 lines called "Reiter über den Bodensee" by Gustav Schwab. It tells of a horseman who is on his way to the shore of Lake
Constance (the Bodensee) on a day when a sheet of snow has obliterated every land-
mark. On finally reaching a house and asking how far it is to the lake, he learns that in
reality he has ridden over the treacherous snow-covered ice to the other side of it, and
is lucky to be alive. He breaks into a cold sweat and dies of shock. Tr.

[203] "Dieser Mann kann Mutter werden" [This Man can Become a Mother] in *Heim und
Welt*, No. 38, Hanover, September 22, 1965, 5 f; "Geschlechtsumwandlung" [Sex
Change] in *Der Spiegel*, No. 39, Hamburg, September 19, 1966, 165.

STATUVOLISM (MIND CONTROL)
(Chapter LXIV)

And so, at times, the mind is completely detached from the body by a strong power of imagination or by deep thought, as Celsus relates concerning a priest, who withdrew his mind as often as he would and lay as one dead, so that if anyone pricked or burned him he felt no pain, but continued to lie motionless and without breathing; however, according to his own account, the voices of people shouting loudly sounded distant to him. But we shall have more to say on this subject later.

CELSUS was a famous physician in the period of the emperor Augustus. He followed the teachings of HIPPOCRATES of Cos (460–377) and was called "the Cicero of Medicine" because of the purity of his literary style. The priest in question was RESTI-TUTUS of Calama, and Agrippa comes back to him in chapter 50 of his Third Book; he is also mentioned by the Church father Aurelius AUGUSTINUS [St. Augustine] (A.D. 354–430) in his *De Civitate Dei* [The City of God] (XIV, 24).

Suspension of the ability to feel pain by a deliberately induced abstraction of the mind is the aim and method of the "Statuvolism" or "willed frame of mind" publicized by Dr. William BAKER-FAHNESTOCK (1804–1894?). The term bestowed by him on this type of self-hypnosis or trance is erroneous, however, because it has nothing to do with the will, and everything to do with the imagination.

The procedure is this: one lies down and, after shutting the eyes, lets the muscles relax, paying no attention to any bodily sensations that may arise, and visits in thought some particularly interesting person in order to see what they are doing and to hear what they are saying. During the first visit, a third party must be present to bring the Statuvolicist gradually back to wakefulness.[204] In addition to anesthesia, the following phenomena can occur: clairvoyance, clairaudience, and in extreme cases

---

[204] William Baker-Fahnestock, *Statuvolism; or Artificial Somnambulism; hitherto called Mesmerism or Animal Magnetism, etc.,* Chicago, 1871, S. Jones; Gregor Konstantin Wittig, *Statuvolence od. der gewollte Zustand und sein Nutzen als Heilmittel in Krampfzuständen und bei Krankheiten des Geistes und Körpers* [Statuvolism or the Willed Frame of Mind and its Use as a Means of Cure in Spasms and in Diseases of the Mind and Body],

bilocation (one's double appearing in another place). Finally there is a danger of "spirit control" involved in the practice—or, to spell it out in plain English, the risk of being possessed by a spirit being, so that we cannot recommend this method unreservedly.

Mary BAKER-EDDY (1821–1910) said in *Science and Health* that if one turns away from and forgets the body by becoming absorbed in something intensely interesting, then one does not suffer pain. Many saints and witches have confirmed the truth of this under torture! Therefore what produces the effect is abandonment to an "over-riding idea." The existence of the "overriding idea" cannot be denied: for the sucking child, it is the baby's bottle. Leave an infant unfed for a day and then present it with its beloved rubber teat, and one can perform minor operations on the starving child without anesthesia as it drinks greedily, and there are no signs that any pain is felt—because "its mind is elsewhere." For lovers, the most glorious thing in the world is the partner. One April evening in 1952, the train from Visselhövede to Walsrode was obliged to stop on the open track because a pair of lovers sitting on the rails had failed to hear the roar and whistling of the engine. "It was only when the engineer climbed down and shouted 'Get off the track!' that he (aged 18) and she (aged 16) awoke from their oblivion to self."[205] For an old woman, knitting can be the absorbing interest, *ne plus ultra,* that distracts her mind from everything else. On a winter's night in 1950 "a woman living in the Altötting district (of Upper Bavaria) put her cold feet into the hot baking-oven in her stove and settled down to her knitting. She failed to notice the smoke that gradually began to curl out of the oven. Only when she felt agonizing pain in her feet did she discover that she was suffering from major(!) burns. The knitter had to go to the doctor."[206]

---

204 Con't
Leipzig, 1884; G. W. Geßmann, *Aus übersinnlicher Sphäre* [From the Supernatural Sphere], Leipzig 1929; 79–85; Johs Guttzeit, *Die Macht des Glaubens und des Willens* [The Power of Faith and of the Will], Leipzig, 1897, 9 (This author coined a preferable definition: "the introspective frame of mind"); Willy Schrödter, "Der gewollte Zustand" [The Willed Frame of Mind], in *Okkulte Stimme,* Part 30, Brunswick, July, 1953, 21 f.

205 "Das Grüne Blatt," No. 15, Dortmund, April 13 (reader's letter from Eitzendf.), 1952, 14.

206 "Westerwälder Post," No. 231, December 5 ("She was too absorbed"), Montabaur, 1950, 7.

"Johannes HUS (1369–1415), when being burned at the stake, was so absorbed in the contemplation of God that his soul was completely withdrawn from his body and he felt no pain (while his flesh was being scorched by the flames), and it is a well-known fact that he calmly sang inspired spiritual songs until a gust of wind blew so much smoke into his face that he was suffocated."[207] In China the art of deliberately switching off pain through thought abstraction is taught in a peculiar sytem of Yoga.[208]

THE POWER OF MENTAL PASSIONS
(Chapter LXV)

When powerful, the passions of the soul, which follow the fantasy, not only can alter the individual's own body but can extend their influence to the bodies of others . . . so as to cause or cure either bodily or mental diseases. . . . The passions of the soul are the main causes of our physical state of health. A strongly elevated soul, under the stimulus of a lively imagination, bestows good or ill health not only on one's own body but also on the bodies of others.

We are surprised to find a number of ultra-modern insights expressed here: the interrelationship between mind (Greek: *psyche*) and body (Greek: *soma*), known as psychosomatic, which reveals the primary cause of "mind-cures"! In this partnership the mind is primary, a truth expressed by the American physician Dr. Sheldon LEAVITT (1848–1933) in the words: "At its inception every

---

[207] Hans Arnold, *Wie man Kranke heilt durch Hypnotismus, Magnetismus und Statuvolence* [How the Sick are Cured by Hypnotism, Magnetism, and Statuvolism], Leipzig, 1907, 52.

[208] Baron von der Goltz, "Zauberei und Hexenkünste, Spiritismus und Schamanismus in China" [Sorcery and Witchcraft, Spiritism and Shamanism in China], in *Mitteilungen der Deutschen Gesellschaft für Natur- und Völkerkunde* [Proceedings of the German Society for Science and Ethnology], vol. VI, Part 51, Tokio, 1893, 8 f; Willy Schrödter, "Okkultismus im Reich der Mitte" [Occultism in the Middle Kingdom (China)], in *Mensch und Schicksal,* No. 8, Villach, July 1, 1953, 7; "Okkultismus im Reich der Mitte" [Occultism in the Middle Kingdom (China)], in *Natur und Kultur,* Series 1, München-Solln, March, 1963, 50.

disease is a psychosis"[209] The feelings change the blood and the other bodily fluids, but first and foremost the blood itself —that "special juice."

The work is done not by a mere thought-picture, but by a thought-picture supported by a sense of excitement.[210] We might call it "meditative ecstasy." Everyday experience teaches us that the "supporting sense of excitement" is usually anxiety, or "enemy number one," and therefore the results are mostly negative.[211] But there is no need for this!

A word may be added here from the Viennese "dietician of the psyche," Baron Ernst von FEUCHTERSLEBEN (1806–1849), "we shall pay for it, if we expose the sensitive surface of our being to the world—but we shall preserve ourselves from harm if we oppose it with active phantasy."[212] "Active phantasy" is what the old masters of wisdom called "imagination" in contrast to "wool-gathering"; in other words, planning one's mental output instead of abandoning oneself to its vagaries.

The influence exercised on a third party is due to what spiritual healers call "resonance," a transfer of emotion; as when two pianos occupy adjacent rooms and, when a note is struck on one, the corresponding string in the other begins to vibrate also."[213] Even Agrippa knew about resonance. In chapter XXIII of Book Two he writes: ". . . Just as in two strings of a lyre stretched to the same extent and in tune with one another, as soon as one is plucked the other vibrates without being touched."[214]

---

[209] Sheldon, Leavitt, *Wege zur Höhe* [The Way Up], Stuttgart, 1909, 239.

[210] Emile Coué, *Die Selbstbemeisterung durch bewußte Autosuggestion,* Basel (Bâle), 1924, [Self-Mastery through Conscious Autosuggestion], Sun Publishers, Santa Fe, NM, 1981; Charles Baudoin, *Suggestion und Autosuggestion* [Suggestion and Autosuggestion], Dresden, 1922; Kurt Rado, *Seelische Hemmungen* [Mental Inhibitions]. Kampen auf Sylt, 1930, 27 f.

[211] L. M. Westall, *Die rationelle psychische Heilmethode* [The Rational Method of Psychic Healing], Leipzig, 1911, 25 f., 32 f., 37 f; Willy Schrödter, *Die Macht der Einbildungskraft* [The Power of Imagination], in *Okk. Stimme,* Part 34, Nov./Part 35 for December, Brunswick, 1953, Parts 1, 2, 3 for January/February/March, Brunswick, 1954, Parts 11 & 12 for November/December, Brunswick, 1957, Parts 1 & 2 for January/February, Brunswick, 1958.

[212] E. Frh. v. Feuchtersleben, *Zur Diätetik der Seele.* Halle/S., 1910, 28 (Gesenius edition).

[213] Dresser, 21; Willy Schrödter, *Präsenzwirkung,* chapter on "Naturkraftsmethode," 78.

[214] Willy Schrödter, *Geheimnisse der Düfte, Farben, Töne* [Secrets of Scent, Color, and Tone], Freiburg, 1963.

TELEPATHY BETWEEN HUMANS AND ANIMALS
(Chapter LXV)

According to Avicenna, a camel may be made to fall if, while desiring that it would do so, one calls on the power of imagination.

This great Muhammadan sage said: "If the mind vividly imagines the fall of an animal, all that is necessary is for the person to fall, too," and Marsilius FICINUS [Ficino] (1433–1499) picks up the same idea in his *Tractatus de Viribus Imaginationis,* that of causing a distant rider to be thrown by a horse into a well. There is an Arab proverb along the same lines: "Allah casts man and camel into the pit by a glance."[215]

I have given examples of telepathy of this sort between humans and animals in my book on "Animal Secrets,"[216] with particular reference to dogs, which may truly be called the "delegated unconscious" of their owners.[217] The Budapest medical hypnotist of European repute, Dr. Franz (Ferenc) VÖLGYESI (born in 1895), exclaims: "How many mysteries still lie hidden in the telepathic and other influences that can be radiated from human to human, animal to animal, and human to animal (or *vice versa*) . . . of which the resonance between radio transmitters and receivers . . . is a very clear and accurate illustration!"[218]

Our author is also supported by "doctor mirabilis" Roger BACON (1214–1294): *Quod si ulterius anima maligna cogitat fortiter de infectione alterius, atque ardenter desideret et certitudinaliter intendat, atque vehementer consideret se posse nocere, non est dubium quin natura obediet cogitationibus animae.*[219] That is to say: "Wherefore, furthermore, if a spiteful person meditates very strongly on harming another, and ardently desires it, concentrates on it with determination, and is absolutely convinced that he can injure him, it is not to be doubted that nature will obey the thoughts of his mind."

---

[215] A case in point is mentioned by Eira Hellberg (born in 1848) in her book *Telepathie-Okkulte Kräfte* [Telepathy—Occult Forces], Prien/Upper Bavaria, 1922, 153. A black magician operating from a distance made a lady fall from her bicycle.

[216] Willy Schrödter, *Tier-Geheimnisse* [Animal Secrets], 131 f, chapter on "Animals and Telepathy."

[217] Dr. Herbert Fritsche, *Tierseele und Schöpfungsgeheimnis* [The Animal Soul and the Secret of Creation], Leipzig, 1940, 190.

[218] Franz Völgyesi, *Menschen- und Tierhypnose* [Hypnosis in Humans and Animals], Zürich & Leipzig, 1938, 29.

[219] Roger Bacon, *Opus majus,* London, 1733, 252.

MATERNAL IMPRESSIONS
(Chapter LXV)

Many monsters are due to the grotesque fancies of pregnant women, as in an example from Pietra Santa, a place in the district of Pisa, related by Marcus Damascenus. It was there that Karl, the emperor, and king of Bohemia, was presented with a girl who came into the world with her body completely covered in hair like a wild animal, because her mother, when pregnant, used to gaze with religious awe on a picture of St. John the Baptist hanging near her bed.

Today we can "no longer deny" those cases "in which the effect of maternal fantasy on the fetus can be verified. The most trustworthy observers from Charles Robert DARWIN (1809–1882) through Ambroise-Auguste LIEBAULT (1823–1904) have produced the most precise and indeed classical evidence for it."[220]

A modern counterpart to Agrippa's example, and one whom older people may well have seen at German fairs, was the subject of this report in 1909: "Lionel, the lion man employed by the Haase side-show company of Leipzig, causes a sensation everywhere, and was certainly the most notable person at the Hamburg Christmas Fair. The 17 year-old, who otherwise is physically and mentally normal, has a lion's mane flowing from his nose, face, and head down over his shoulders; his back, too, is covered in long hair, which is less thick on his chest and arms, but his hands are free. His mother is said to have witnessed the terrible scene in which her husband, the animal trainer belonging to a traveling circus in Russia, was badly mauled one morning while taming a lion. Seven months later this boy came into the world completely covered in hair. Needless to say, this is an outstanding 'maternal impressions' case.[221]

Nevertheless, probably the most outstanding of all such cases is the following, in which the maternal impression of an ancestress has been passed down through the generations to the present day: "On the night of New Year's Eve in 1505, the Dutch

---

[220] Baudoin, 95, given names and dates supplied by W. Schr.
[221] A. K., "Kurze Notizen," [Brief Notes], in *Psychische Studien,* Part 2, Leipzig, February, 1909, 121; Carl Zuckmayer, *Die Fastnachtsberichte* [Carnival News], Frankfurt/M., 1959, 126 f.

Burgomaster Haanappel (of Doesburg), suddenly noticed that the church tower was on fire. As he was rushing to the church, he saw to his dismay that the flames had already caught hold of the beams supporting the roof. At the last moment he seized the bell-rope just as the floor collapsed and plunged into the crypt. Haanappel clung to the rope and let himself swing to and fro like the tongue of a bell until the bell itself began to toll. When the townsfolk entered the church, they found their Burgomaster lying unconscious on the flagstones. The inner surfaces of his hands were burned and the skin hung from them in ribbons. When a son was born to him and his wife two years later, the baby's hands displayed exactly the same black burn marks as his father had. Ever since—for the last 450 years—all Haanappel descendants (and the family is still living in the Dutch town of Doesburg) have been born with the inner surfaces of their hands black."[222]

Dermagraphism, in which a mental image copies itself on the skin of the one who is actually doing the visualizing, may be regarded as a less advanced stage of maternal impressions [in which there is a transfer to another person, i.e., the child, Tr.]. Here is an example given by the physiologist Charles RICHET (1850–1935), Nobel prize winner in 1913: "A mother watching her playing child removing the sharp-pointed pot-hook from over the stove, realizes that it can easily fall and hit his head. The thought pierces her to the marrow, and immediately there appears on her own neck, at the very place where the child would be struck, a red weal, which lasts for several hours."[223]

> This sort of thing is not confined to humans; it also occurs in irrational animals. Thus we read of the patriarch Jacob that he made the color of Laban's sheep variegated by means of [speckled] rods laid in water. ... Thus the imagination of peacocks and other brooding birds impresses their colors on the feathers, so that we can breed white peacocks if the cages where they are brooding are hung with white linen sheets.

---

[222] André Sonnet, *Der Mensch ist voller Geheimnisse: Im Bereich des Unerklärlichen* [Human Beings are Full of Mysteries: In the Realm of the Inexplicable], Berlin Grunewald, 1959, 31.
[223] Baudoin, 103.

To those who cannot bring themselves to believe that the higher animals possess any imagination, we would say that "many owners of pedigree bitches observe phantom pregnancies several times a year."[224]

Maternal impressions in animals are an acknowledged fact. Researchers found that a bruise on the hind leg of a mother animal had conjured up a corresponding stripe-shaped contusion on the hind leg of the embryo, and that after several brain operations on a pregnant dam, the embryos exhibited blood-stained lesions in the same area of the skull. The "knowledge books" of the Renaissance seized on Jacob's method [Genesis 30: 31–43. Tr.] and extended it to horses: recommending that mares should be covered by stallions while standing on mats of the color desired for the foals.[225] To this might be added an observation made by STARK: a pair of pouter-pigeons, one of whose newly hatched chicks had died, had a drum-pigeon put in the nest as a replacement and proceeded to rear it. Meanwhile more pouter-pigeon eggs were laid. When these were hatched, the young resembled the foster-bird and not their own parents.[226]

PERSONAL INFLUENCE
(Chapter LXV)

It is well-known that the body is very easily infected by the fumes from another's diseased body, as may be clearly seen in the plague and in leprosy. . . . Therefore no one should be astonished that the body and mind of one person can be similarly affected by the mind of another, since the mind is far more powerful, strong, fervent, and mobile than any fumes exhaled by the body;

---

[224] Herb Fritsche, *Tierseele und Schöpfungsgeheimnis* [The Animal Soul and the Secret of Creation], Leipzig, 1940, 300.

[225] E. Hch. Fischer, *Albertus Magnus, der Andere u. Wahre, etc.* [Albertus Magnus, the Pseudo and the Genuine, etc.], Altona & Leipzig, 1790, 327.

[226] Anonymous, *Die Tyroler ekstat. Jungfrauen, Leitsterne i.d. dunklen Gebiete der Mystik* [The Ecstatic Virgins of the Tyrol, Guiding Stars in the Dark Domain of Mysticism], chapter on the stigmata and on mystical mimicry and physiological plasticity in general), Regensburg, 1843, vol. II, 284–289.

nor does it lack the means by which to operate. Besides, an alien soul can surely have no less power over the body than an alien body has. And so we find that one individual may act on another purely by temperament and character.

"The cultural history of all times and regions tells of those who are able to exercise a healthy or an unhealthy influence on their surroundings—in the widest sense—merely by their silent and outwardly inactive presence. As our use of the word 'inactive' implies, we are not talking about someone inspiring others by setting them an example, but about the infectiousness of what radiates from a personality possessing a certain psychic structure."[227]

For just as asafoetida and musk permeate everything with their smell, so something evil is transferred from the evil to those nearby, and something good from the good, and often it clings to them for a long time. . . . Therefore the philosophers warn us not to associate with evil-minded and miserable individuals, because their psyches, being filled with harmful radiations, infect their surroundings in an unwholesome way. Conversely, one should seek the company of good and successful people, for these can be very beneficial to us by their vicinity.

The application of the above truth to therapy gives this result:

In addition to the effect of the active principle in the medicine, there is the effect of the power of mind of the physician, which is strong enough to give a new direction to the sick body, especially when the patient has confidence in the doctor and thus is self-conditioned to receive the virtue of the doctor as well as that of his remedies (chapter LXVI).

---

[227] Willy Schrödter, *Präsenzwirkung*, 15.

If we translate his words into up-to-date language, the "demonic knight" anticipates that the patient will be tuned, through "meditative resonance" (Gemassmer), to the normal vibration rates of the healer: rectification, synchronization, syntonization, consonance, priming, or healing impulse imparted to the sick person's disturbed entelechy!

"In brief," says Dr. Francesco RACANELLI of Florence (born in 1904), a modern physician and mesmerist, as he echoes Agrippa's thoughts on the subject (the 'retuning' of the patient by the doctor), "the doctor operates mainly by his personal influence, by that positive, imponderable 'something' which flows out from him to the patient as a whole, and, by this therapeutic process, he strengthens the medicinal treatment, regardless of whether the latter happens to be in the field of so-called 'orthodox' or 'illegal' medicine."[228] Using many examples, and quoting many sources, I have dealt with this theme (so important to us all) of the effect of forceful natures on their environment in a monograph titled *History of Energy Transference.*[229]

In his Third Book, chapter 48, our mage reverts to this topic and quotes from tradition to show that the force field accompanying a "supercharged" personality can affect the intellect of others as well as their characters and health:

> *In the* Book of Senators *in the section called Eleazar we read that Rabbi Jochanaan ben Jochai so illuminated an uneducated peasant named Eleazar that he— being bathed in a sudden splendor—unexpectedly recited such profound secrets of the Torah in the congregation of the wise that all present were astonished.*

A modern example of the same sort is when pilgrims streamed to the Indian holy man Bhagwan Sri RAMANA Maharishi (1879–1950) in Tiruvannamalai (South India), "not to hear or see anything, but in order to be able to meditate more easily than they otherwise could in the atmosphere of the master, and

---

[228] Francesco Racanelli, *Gabe des Heilens* [The Gift of Healing], München-Planegg, 1953, 75.
[229] Willy Schrödter, *Präsenzwirkung,* 110.

perhaps to be irradiated by his enlightenment, too."[230] Obviously a company (Agrippa uses the word "choir") of powerful, highly-developed humans is bound to produce powerful effects in any percipients (receivers) on whom it directs its attention.

> In the Holy Scriptures we read of Saul that, as long as he was among the prophets, the Spirit of the Lord came upon him and he prophesied; but when he left the company of the sons of the prophets he ceased to prophesy.[231]
> The same thing happened to the messengers sent by Saul to arrest David; when they caught sight of the Choir of the prophets with Samuel presiding over them, the Spirit of God came on them and they prophesied too.[232]

Then follows the insight concerning the overflow from powerful natures to normal individuals:

> *Apparently, in prophets seized by divine inspiration the plenitude of light is often so great that people in their immediate neighborhood are also seized by it and become driven by a similar spirit.*

FAITH AS A MAGICAL AGENT
(Chapter LXVI)

> *Much is achieved by our mind through faith, which is a firm belief, a fixed intention, and a complete absorption of the operator or recipient, and it assists in every matter and lends strength to every deed we wish to do; so that what may be called an image is formed inside us of the power to be assimilated and of the thing to be performed in us or by us. Therefore in every work and application we must employ a strong desire, must*

---

[230] Dr. Hans-Hasso von Veltheim-Ostrau, *Der Atem Indiens* [The Spirit of India], Hamburg, 1954, 256 f.
[231] I Samuel 10: 10–13.
[232] I Samuel 19: 20–21.

stretch our imagination, and must have the most san-
guine hope and the firmest faith, for this contributes
very much to success. . . .
Thus in order to perform magic, firm faith and un-
bounded confidence are required; there must not be the
slightest doubt of success or the least thought of fail-
ure. For just as, even on those occasions when the
wrong procedure is used, a firm and unshakeable faith
can do wonders,[233] *so every misgiving and scruple dis-*
pels and breaks the mental force of the operator,[234] *who*
falls between two stools. And so the desired influence
is not obtained but miscarries, since it cannot fasten
on, or unite with, things or actions without the fixed
and unshakeable force of the soul.

This deep insight requires no commentary; the words are golden
to the budding mage.[235] In his next chapter (LXVII), Agrippa pro-
vides equally correct information on the efficient (Latin: *agens*)
magical "vehicles," such as sigils and spells:

The philosophers, especially the Arabs, say that when
the human soul with its emotions and inclinations is
much absorbed in a work, it binds itself to the souls of
the stars and to the intelligences. This binding brings
it about that a certain wonderful force flows into
things and our operations. Partly because the soul
knows everything and can do everything, partly be-
cause things are inclined to obey it, and partly because
things are naturally active and tend to move in the di-
rection the soul most ardently desires. . . . And this is
what underlies the effectiveness of letters, images,
magic spells, certain words and many other marvel-
lous experiments.

---

[233] In the Chinese Yoga Book of the Elixir of Life we read: "When the right man (white
magician) makes use of the wrong means, the wrong means work in the right way,"
and then "But if the wrong man uses the right means, the right means work in the
wrong way." (Richard Wilhelm and C. G. Jung, *The Secret of The Golden Flower,* Rout-
ledge & Kegan Paul, London, 1979, 63.)

[234] Paracelsus says exactly the same: "Any doubt ruins the work, which would otherwise be quite certain."

[235] Willy Schrödter, *Offenbarungen eines Magiers* [The Revelations of a Magician], Warpke-Billerbeck, 1955.

*Therefore everything intended by the soul of some-
one deeply in love has a strong effect in love affairs, and
everything intended by the soul of someone nursing a
grudge is capable of causing harm and destruction.
And the same is true of anything the soul passionately
desires.*

*So everything done and dictated, whether letters,
figures, words, sentences, gestures, or the like, rein-
forces the will, and acquires marvelous powers if the
soul of the operator has reached a high pitch of desire
and is under a favorable aspect and influence of the
stars. When our soul is carried away by some excessive
emotion or virtue, it often chooses of its own accord the
best, most effective, and most suitable hour or opportunity. . . . Thus the great emotions in the things dictated
by the soul at such an hour, are accompanied by many
wonderful powers producing astounding effects.*

STELLAR INVOCATION
(Chapter LXXI)

*In composing songs and prayers to attract the power of
a star or of some higher being, one must pay due regard
to the powers, effects, and functions belonging to that
star, and must eulogize, elevate and commend its en-
dowments and influences in the songs. On the other
hand, whatever needs to be destroyed and prevented
has to be disparaged and condemned; we must beg and
implore for what we wish to obtain, and must de-
nounce and execrate what we want destroyed and prevented.*

*The words of these songs must be fine and elegant,
and the versification and style must match the occasion. What is more, we are told by magicians to address
the star or higher being for whom the song is intended
by its name, its wonders, its movements and the course
it takes in its sphere, by its light, dignity, beauty and
brightness, by its strength and marvelous powers, and
so on.*

In chapter LIX of Book Two, we read:

> *But anyone who wants a more detailed knowledge of invocations of the stars and planets and wishes to research the matter more thoroughly, should turn to the Orphic hymns; for whoever properly understands these has gained a deep insight into natural magic.*[236]

Stellar invocations assume that the stars and planets have souls—a topic to which we shall return later. Even today, there are isolated individuals who make this assumption and suppose that these stellar souls may be effectively evoked.

---

[236] See also Willy Schrödter, *A Rosicrucian Notebook*, Samuel Weiser, York Beach, ME, 1992; Schrödter, *Astral-Mystik* [Astral mysticism], Pforzheim, 1958, 12 f; G. A. van Rijnberk, *Épisodes de la Vie ésotérique* [Episodes in the Esoteric Life], Lyon, n.d., 133 (Derain); Ernst Maaß, *Orpheus,* Munich, 1895 (Beck).

SECOND BOOK

ON CELESTIAL MAGIC

But if by magic you mean a perpetual research amongst all that is more latent and obscure in nature, I answer, I profess that magic, and that he who does so comes but nearer to the fountain of all belief.

Lord Edward George BULWER-LYTTON (1803–1873)
Zanoni (1843, Book the Second, chapter 7)

MAGIC LANTERN AND PERISCOPE
(Chapter I)

So too transparent mirrors are made which, when coated with certain vegetable juices and illuminated by artificial light, fill the surrounding air with amazing phantasms. I myself know how to align mirrors in such a way that one can see very clearly at a distance of several miles everything that is in the sunlight.

The first-mentioned piece of optical apparatus would seem to be a primitive magic lantern such as is commonly said to have been invented by the Jesuit professor Athanasius KIRCHER (1601–1680). Usually the slides were projected on smoke rising from a censer and, in keeping with the spirit of the age, they were known as "ghostly apparitions." It is worth recalling here what Agrippa said in chapter 6 of Book One about "certain mirrors" (concave mirrors?) "by which any images one pleases can be produced in the air in such a way that those who are not in the know think they are seeing spirits or the shades of the departed"!

Thus Agrippa's teacher—TRITHEMIUS—showed the Emperor Maximilian I the "shade" of his dead wife Maria von Burgundy (born 1457, married 1477, died 1482). However ca. 100 B.C. the Taoist sorcerer WANG exhibited in the same way his deceased mistress to the emperor Han Wu-Ti (140–87 B.C.). On the other hand, from 1782 and onward, Father Johann Adalbert HAHN (1750–1825), the last prebendary of the chapel of the Holy Cross in the mountain town of Platten, "the Doctor Faustus of the Erzgebirge," would trick his peasants into thinking they were seeing ghosts with the help of a magic lantern that he often carried in a knapsack and by the use of ventriloquism.[1] Nevertheless, not all his feats are explicable by his employment of the above methods, but depend on a special hypnosis technique that has been lost in Europe since the Middle Ages: this is instantaneous mass hypnosis (mental suggestion, Hindu hypnotism), which the wizard cleric himself called *ars venetiana*.[2] In my opinion, the second combination of mirrors was a periscope (Greek: *peri* = around, *skopein* = to see), which

---

[1] Prof. Johann Endt, *Sagen und Schwänke a.d. Erzgebirge* [Legends and Amusing Stories from the Erzgebirge. The Wizard Father Hahn, the Folk Doctor Rölz, and others]. Sammlg.: Beitr. z. dt.-böhm. Volkskunde; X. Bd. [An anthology: Contributions to German-Bohemian folklore, vol. X]. Reichenberg, 1925, 5, 21, 38.

[2] Endt, 21.

allows one to look out over the top of an obstruction (such as a trench) and enables the crew of a submarine to know, without surfacing, what is going on above them. But it is possible that a reflector telescope was intended, and we shall be coming back to this later.

THE NUMBER 4 AND ITS SCALE
(Chapter VII)

The number Four is called the Tetraktys by the Pythagoreans. . . . There are four cardinal points: east, west, north, and south. There are four elements under the heavens: fire, air, water, and earth; four primary qualities under the heavens: cold, hot, dry, wet; and through these four humors or temperaments: the sanguine, phlegmatic, choleric, and melancholic. The year is divided into four seasons: spring, summer, fall, and winter; and there are four main winds: east, west, south, and north. Paradise has four rivers and so does the underworld. . . . Also the whole of mathematics is based on four fundamentals: the point, the line, the surface, the solid. . . . For this reason the Pythagoreans swore by the number four . . . this is known as the "Pythagorean oath."

Agrippa appended a "Scale of the Number Four," showing its connection with the four elements. I reproduce the easiest part of this table here as a sample. He drew up similar "scales" for the numbers 1 through 10 and 12. If I have chosen the number four and its scale to represent the rest, it is for a good reason! We might say that the cosmos is bound to a cross. But what does that mean? The cross represents a dis-union: two straight lines intersect, and so to speak cross swords like two fencers trying to settle accounts with one another. The cross with its four open squares takes the form of a QUADRATURE. In the two warring crossbars we can see the two primeval polarities. If we do not wish to make of them anything as abstract as action and reaction or positive and negative forces (after the analogy of the Chinese YANG and YIN), we may at least view them, with Carl BUTTENSTEDT (1845-1910), as tension and relaxation.[3]

---
[3] Buttenstedt, 13.

Freemasonry has the pillars Jachin and Boaz [mentioned in the Bible] as symbols of this. These are also copied in Würzburg Cathedral (Lagutt)—dating from 1260. As long as nature formed (*natura naturata*) and nature formative (*natura naturans*)[4] exist, the creative conflict between the primeval contraries will not cease. Or, to put it another way, at the instant they ceased, the manifest universe would come to an end, and everything would be swallowed up in the creative ONE (Chinese: *Wu-Gi*; Hebrew: *Ain Soph*), of which the dyad (Greek: *dyas*) is simply the bifurcation (forking), or "Y," of PYTHAGORAS (580–493).

An essential feature of the cosmic struggle is that neither of the primeval antagonists gains a lasting victory over the other but, as soon as either of them gains a temporary advantage, the effort and advance are followed by a relaxation and retreat. Thus the two polarized forces are always passing through the two phases of their struggle and exhibit a low (minimum) or a high (maximum), an ebb or a flow. The two antagonists in their two periods produce a QUATERNARY (Greek: *tetraktys;* Latin: *quaternar*), which, when formed into a "scheme of correspondences" makes possible a sort of "higher equations." We encounter a table of this kind back in Ancient Greece,[5] but only the "sur-éminent disciple" [*supereminent disciple*] (so SEDIR calls him) of the ROSI-CRUCIANS, the court counsellor of the elector of Bavaria, Carl von ECKARTSHAUSEN (1752–1803), who was at home in the mysteries, has transmitted to us a helpful discovery.[6] Using his terms expansion and contraction for the primal antagonists, I now repeat a simplified "periodic table" of the traditional elements.[7] I believe these examples are enough to show the type of tabulation that can help one to gain some very useful insights when using Table 1, The Magic Key of Analogy (NOVALIS). See page 102.

---

[4] *Natura naturans—natura naturata:* "Nature formative—nature formed." The two ultimate principles of the Dualistic Philosophy are technically so called. H. T. Riley, ed.: *A Dictionary of Classical Quotations.* George Bell & Sons, London, 1876, 246. Tr. note.

[5] Robert Henseling, *Umstrittenes Weltbild* [Controversial Cosmogony], Leipzig, 1939, 114.

[6] C. v. Eckartshausen, *Aufschlüsse zur Magie, etc.* [Elucidations of Magic, etc.], Munich, 1790; Hans Sterneder, *Frühling im Dorf* [Spring in the Village], Leipzig, 1929, 224–225.

[7] Willy Schrödter, "Zahlenlehre der Natur" [Nature's Arithmetic] in *Der Spiegel*, Freiburg/Brsg., 1938, 167 f. *Streifzug ins Ungewohnte* [A Trip into the Unusual], chapter titled "The Primal Antagonists, their Phases and Correspondences," Freiburg/Brsg, 1949, 163 f.

Table 1. The Magic Key of Analogy.

	אש Fire	רוח Air	מים Water	עפר Earth	
The four elements	Fire	Air	Water	Earth	In the
The four qualities	Heat	Wetness	Coldness	Dryness	world
The four seasons	Summer	Spring	Winter	Fall	of the
The four cardinal points	East	West	North	South	elements
Four sorts of mixed bodies	Animals	Vegetables	Metals	Stones	where
Four types of animal	Walking	Flying	Swimming	Crawling	the law
Correspondences of the elements in plants	Seeds	Flowers	Leaves	Roots	of
Correspondences of the elements in metals	Gold and iron	Copper and tin	Mercury	Lead and silver	generation
Correspondences of the elements in stones	Sparkling and full of fire	Light and transparent	Lustrous and hard	Heavy and opaque	and decay is in
The four elements in humans	Intellect	Spirit	Soul	Body	force

Table 2. Contraction and Expansion.

EXPANSION INCREASING	EXPANSION (maximum) CONTRACTION (minimum)
Waxing moon	Full moon
Spring	Summer
Morning	Noon
East	South
Child	Adult
Surface	Solid
Wet	Hot
Vegetable	Animal
Sanguine	Choleric
Cheerfulness	Exuberance
Walking animal	Flying animal
Sparkling stones	Transparent stones
Growth	Life
CONTRACTION INCREASING	CONTRACTION (maximum) EXPANSION (minimum)
Waning moon	New moon
Fall	Winter
Evening	Night
West	North
Old age	Fetus
Line	Point
Dry	Cold
Metals	Stones
Melancholic	Phlegmatic
Dullness	Sloth
Swimming animals	Crawling animals
Lustrous stones	Opaque stones
Disease	Death

The Chinese have constructed a "scheme of relationships" on a fivefold basis (a quinternary).[8] See Table 2, above. Since their philosophy of life is based on two opposing forces, one cannot help wondering why they, too, did not arrive at a fourfold division![9]

[8] Dr. Jean Marquès-Rivière, *Amulettes, Talismans et Pentacles* [Amulets, Talismans and Pentacles], Paris, 1938, 205; Maximilian Kern, *Das Licht des Ostens* [The Light from the East], Stuttgart, n.d., 273.

[9] Schrödter, *Grenzw. Versuche* [Paranormal Research for All], 288 f. (The "Yin-Yang" Symbol).

THE IMPORTANCE OF PROPER NAMES
(Chapter XX)

According to the Pythagoreans (and the followers of Aristotle and Ptolemy agree with them) certain divine numbers underlie the letters of the alphabet, so that we can derive hidden information and can foretell the future from the proper names of things. . . . This type of divination is known as numerology because it is performed with numbers.

This Kabbalah of numbers is still popular[10] and often yields astonishing results. But there is more to come! Agrippa continues:

Terence[11] refers to it in the following verses:

> *The proper names have numbers all*
> *And some are large while some are small.*
> *This sways the fortunes of a fight;*
> *The larger number wins the day,*
> *The smaller warns of death they say:*
> *Patroclus fell by Hector's blow,*
> *Achilles then laid Hector low.*

Pliny records an assertion by Pythagoras that an uneven number of vowels in given names would cure lameness, blindness, and similar disabilities when the members on the right side of the body are affected, and that an even number of vowels would do the same when those on the left side of the body are affected.

According to this, the choice of names is important for the health and welfare of an individual. John Godolphin BENNETT (born in 1897) relates of the Indonesian spiritual teacher SUBUH (born in 1901): "According to custom, his father chose his name and called him Sukarno. The child fell sick and for several days could not take food. His death seemed inevitable and the women of

---

[10] Hans Müller, *Der Mensch im Kraftfeld kosm. Faktoren* (Humans in the Forcefield of Cosmic Factors], Pforzheim, 1959.

[11] Marcus Terentianus, Latin grammarian, mystic and poet of the late second century.

the house were wailing their laments, when an old man passing by asked the reason, and on being told that a child was dying, asked his name. He said that the name was wrongly chosen and that he should be called Muhammad Subuh. His father accordingly changed his name and, from that moment, the child began to take food and grew up strong and healthy."[12] *Pak* (Indonesian for "father") SUBUH has often changed the given names of his SUBUD adherents. However these name changes are too recent for any conclusion to be reached on their possible effectiveness.

GOETHE was aware of the significance of names. When, on one occasion, Johann Gottfried von HERDER (1744–1803) speculated whether his name signified that he was descended from the Goths or had some other meaning, he replied, "A person's proper name is not like a cloak that hangs loosely round him, but is like a body-hugging garment that fits as tight as a second skin."

My school friends and I were under the same impression, and we made a game of it by guessing a schoolmate's given names from his physiognomy and behavior, and I cannot remember that we were ever far wrong. Of course, telepathy may have played a part. Later on I read in Georg Christoph LICHTENBERG (1742–1799): "I ask all physiognomists if they have never guessed given names from faces; Kaspar is term of abuse in many districts." Alfred TENNYSON (1809–1892) attained a state of so-called "Cosmic Consciousness" (Dr. Bucke) when he mentally repeated his own name over and over again.[13]

REFLECTOR TELESCOPE
(Chapter XXIII)

I myself know how to do amazing things through them and to make mirrors in which anyone can see anything he wishes from a very long way away.

One is reminded here of the reflector telescope invented in 1671 by Sir Isaac NEWTON (1643–1727), in which the focal image is formed by a concave mirror instead of by an objective (lens). The

---

[12] J. G. Bennett, *Concerning Subud*, University Books, New York, 1959, 53–54.
[13] Willy Schrödter, *Abenteuer mit Gedanken* [Adventures with Thoughts], chapter on Haunting Oneself, 11–12.

largest instrument of this type is to be found on Mount Palomar (California) and was designed by George E. HALE [1869–1938] and Albert EINSTEIN (1879–1955).

It has a 200-inch mirror and the block of glass from which this was ground weighed 20 tons. The aperture of the telescope is 10 inches and, with a range of 1 billion light years, it is a million times stronger than the human eye. It moves on a ten-story high, electrically operated bearing. The observatory is situated on a plateau at the top of the 6125 foot mountain.

Earlier in the chapter, AGRIPPA has asserted:

Whoever knows the properties of these [geometrical] *plane and solid figures, as well as their interdependence, can perform many wonders in natural magic and in perspective, especially with mirrors.*

This reminds us of a remark by ECKARTSHAUSEN: "Some incredible things of which our physicists do not even dream are still hidden in optics. Just consider the concave mirror and the burning glass"![14] Think again of the hall of mirrors, which conjures up the metaphysics of optics before our very eyes![15]

Perhaps in the foreseeable future someone will invent a mechanical tube like the one which the Chaldean adept MEJNOUR said to his English neophyte Clarence Glyndon would "discover the nobler and more gifted things that hover in the illimitable air" because "in space there are millions of beings, not literally spiritual, for they have all, like the animalculae unseen by the naked eye, certain forms of matter so delicate, air-drawn, and subtle, that it is, as it were, but a film, a gossamer that clothes the spirit."[16]

---

[14] Carl von Eckartshausen, *Mystische Nächte* ("Vierte Nacht") [Mystic nights: Night Four], Munich, 1788.

[15] Heinrich Jürgens, "Spiegelpraxis und Spiegelmagie" [Experiments with Mirrors and Mirror Magic], *Bücher der weißen Fähne*, vol. 27, Pfullingen i. Wttbg, n.d., ca. 1920; Maya Para, *Die Macht der Spiegel (Spiegelmagie)* [The Power of Mirrors (Mirror Magic), Bad Schmiedeberg and Leipzig, 1921; Willy Schrödter, *Vom Hundersten* [One Thing and Another], 163 f.

[16] Lord Edward Bulwer-Lytton, *Zanoni* (Book 4, chap. 4), London, 1845, and reprints; Willy Schrödter, *Abenteuer mit Gedanken* [Adventures with Ideas], 13.

THE POWER OF MUSICAL TONES
(Chapter XXIV)

In inanimate nature: Even the elements rejoice in melodies. The Halesian spring, otherwise quiet and still, bubbles up merrily and overflows its banks at the sound of a flute.

The same phenomenon was reported by an experienced traveler to his friend Prof. Hans STERNEDER (born in 1889)—although he did not name the place—and the professor swears it was no "traveler's tale"; the lady friend of the "wonder apostle" thought that the singing of the human voice, as the noblest instrument of all, must have an even greater effect.[17]

As a matter of fact, in the Sri Lankan jungle there is a sacred spring tasting of soda that is so sensitive to sound that loud speech (and song) makes it bubble. The expedition sent there to find out why this happens did not publish an explanation, however. At all events, when the elephants come to drink they trumpet before dipping in their trunks.[18]

In the animal world: Harmonious music keeps in tune with the heavenly bodies . . . indeed it attracts dumb brutes, serpents, birds, and dolphins, to listen to its melodies. Birds are lured by pipes, and stags are caught by means of them too. . . . In the lake at Alexandria, fish are assembled by clapping. Dolphins are made friendly to humans by the tones of a lute. Northern swans will follow the sound of a zither. The Indian elephant is tamed by organ notes. . . . The Arabs maintain that a laden camel gains strength from the song of its driver.

I have supplied recent examples of the same kind in the section on "music and animals" in my study "Die Magie des Tones" [The Magic of Sound] (*Neue Wissenschaft*, Oberengstringen bei Zürich, annual set 1955, Parts. 8/9, 267 f.).

---

[17] Hans Sterneder, *Frühling im Dorf* [Spring in the Village], Leipzig, 1929, 71 f.
[18] Anonymous, "Natur wunder auf Ceylon" [Prodigies in Ceylon] in *Welt am Sonnabend*, No. 12, Düsseldorf, March 19, 1955, 15.

In humans: Also the influences of the stars are not absent from musical harmony, since it is the supreme pattern-maker of all. When properly adjusted to the heavenly bodies it elicits celestial effects in a marvelous way and alters the mood, intentions, gestures, and movements, as well as the activities and dispositions of the listeners, and suddenly transports them to whatever it is expressing, whether joy or sadness, boldness or composure, etc.

We learn from Robert FLUDD (1574–1637) that the Rosicrucians deliberately operated with combinations of tones which they associated with the astrological aspects.[19] "Thus it is no wonder that the Brothers have been able to draw to themselves princes and potentates by their knowledge and employment of such music."[20] And now the time has come to ask and answer the question, "How is it possible for the distant stars, the constellations Aries, Taurus, Gemini, etc. to influence the development of the psyche? Now no one maintains, on theoretical grounds, that this is what *has to* happen; it is experience that teaches us that this is what *does* happen. In effect, the distant stars resolve themselves into symbolic images of dynamic constellations connected with the annual orbit of Earth around the Sun. And the planets, as siblings of Earth, are involved with it in the dynamics of our solar system—within the tension field of which all terrestrial life exists.[21] AGRIPPA continues:

It calms the mind, elevates the soul, inflames the warrior for battle, lightens labor, consoles misery, raises the fallen and despairing, and refreshes travelers. . . . Those who bear heavy burdens are in the habit of singing and this makes their work easier. Saxo Grammaticus tells, in his "Danish History," of a musician who boasted that he could make people so crazy by his playing that none of the hearers could release themselves

---

[19] Fritz Stege, *Musik—Magie—Mystik* [Music—Magic—Mysticism], Remagen, 1961, 143.
[20] Robert Fludd, *Schutzschrift f. d. Aechtheit der Rosenkreutzergesellschaft* [A Defense of the Genuineness of the Rosicrucian Society], (translated by AdaMah Booz), Leipzig, 1782.
[21] Artur Strauss, "Das Doppelgesicht der Astrologie" [The Double Aspect of Astrology], in *Athena,* No. 11, Berlin, September, 1947, 55 f.

from its spell. When the king ordered him to make good his words, he worked on people's feelings by various melodies and filled the auditors in an unusually solemn way with gloom and horror; then, passing with more lively notes from sobriety to merriment, he transported them to a gleeful frame of mind, and actually inveigled them into making indecent movements and gestures. Finally he deprived his listeners of their senses, by his increasing vehemence, to such a degree that their excitement rose to madness and frenzy.

Now we know of popular songs that have sparked off epidemics of suicide,[22] and of the mass-hysterical riots of rock-and-roll fans constantly reported in the daily press! And one has only to think of Beatlemania to grasp the meaning of that medieval expression —referring to tarantism—*Diabolus in musica* (Latin for "The Devil in Music"), and to understand the proposal of Kung-fu-Tse (Confucius, 551–478) and Plato (427–347) that musicians should be placed under state control.

But listen again to our High Magus:

Timotheus filled king Alexander with fury at will and then calmed him.

In chapter XLVI of Book Three, Agrippa repeats this example; adding another that also shows the power of music over the human soul:

Timotheus is said to have filled Alexander the Great with fury by his playing and, according to the testimony of Aurelius Augustinus, a priest of Calame used to put himself at will into a state of trance and rapture by means of a plaintive melody.

We read again of the same priest, in Book Three, chapter L: "He was laid out without breathing, exactly like a corpse, and felt

---

[22] Willy Schrödter, "Die Magie des Tones" [The Magic of Musical Notes] in *Neue Wissenschaft,* Parts 8/9 (Section on "Humans and Tones"), Oberengstringen bei Zürich, Aug./Sept, 1955.

nothing when burnt or cut." (Cf. Proverbs 23:35: "They have beaten me, and I felt it not"!) In other words, he placed himself in a state of catalepsy by "Statuvolence" and was called "Restitutus." (St. Augustine: *De civitate Dei*, XIV, 23).

Our author, a Faust-like figure of the late Renaissance, "used fasting in conjunction with fumigations and melodies, which he created by dropping lead balls on a stringed instrument, and raised himself by these means to the mental plane, and even had fleeting visions of the divine plane, although the latter were not perfectly clear," according to Baron von KLEE-BERG (born in 1930), a high-ranking Freemason and Martinist (with the lodge name Isiacus) in his unpublished "Diary Notes" (*Rosicruciana* No. 504/23).

Compare with the above how the prophet Elisha (Latin: *Elisaeus*, ca. 850 B.C.) asked, before he started to prophesy, for a minstrel to play to him (II Kings 3:15 f.)! And Dr. Fritz TELTSCHER of Innsbruck (died in 1949), investigator of the "subtle force fluids" caught a glimpse of the "essential crystals" of human beings when he played his accordion!

MUSIC THERAPY
(Chapter XXIV)

Song produces a fresh and cheerful feeling, allays anger, brightens misery and ill-humor, heals divisions, calms the rage of the insane, and dispels unprofitable thoughts. . . . Therefore various physical and mental illnesses can be cured or caused by it, as has been pointed out by Democritus and Theophrastus. Thus we read of how the inhabitants of Lesbos and Ionia were allegedly healed by the music of Terpander and of Arion of Mithimna. Also Ismenias the Theban used music to cure many sufferers. In addition Orpheus, Amphion, David, Pythagoras, Empedocles, Asclepiades, and Timotheus performed many marvels by singing and by playing on musical instruments, sometimes enlivening the low-spirited by popular airs, sometimes checking sensuality, frenzy, and rage by more solemn tones. Thus David soothed the fury of

Saul by playing the harp; Pythagoras rescued a dissolute youth from immorality; Timotheus aroused king Alexander to a fury at will, and calmed him again. . . . Then we read that in Apulia those who have been bitten by a tarantula spider become numb and lie lifeless until they hear a certain melody and start dancing to its beat. This cures them; but long afterward they cannot help dancing as soon as they hear the same notes. According to Gellius, the most acute sciatica can be eased by the sound of a flute, and the same writer, quoting Theophrastus, states that even adder bites can be cured by flute playing, while Democritus says that the sound of this instrument has been used as a remedy for most human diseases.

Here again, for lack of space, I must refer the reader to my short paper and book on the subject;[23] also to the interesting study by the Wiesbaden musical critic, theorist, and composer Dr. Fritz STEGE,[24] from which we can gather that the Tarantella "does not represent music therapy, but is the expression of a dancing epidemic."[25] That opponent of the Rosicrucians, the Jesuit professor Athanasius KIRCHER (1601–1680)—who was very "Rosicrucian" himself, surprisingly enough—states in his *Musurgia* [Musurgia Universalis] that "by means of this art (music), the Rosicrucian Brotherhood are said to have expelled incurable diseases of all sort."[26] At the end of chapter XXVIII of Book Two Agrippa returns to this topic:

The old sages, who possessed an accurate knowledge of the harmonious relationship of mind and body, made skillful use of music and song for preserving and restoring health according to individual dispositions and temperaments, and also for ensuring a more healthy cultivation of the emotions, and for making people more receptive to the heavenly harmony and completely heavenly. . . . Also nothing is more effective

---

[23] Willy Schrödter, *Magie des Tones* [The Magic of Musical Notes], 276 f.
[24] Dr. Fritz Stege, *Musik—Magie—Mystik* [Music—Magic—Mysticism], Remagen, 1961, 233 f.
[25] Stege, 196 f.
[26] Stege, 145 f.

> *than musical harmony for exorcizing evil spirits; for as they have fallen from heavenly harmony they cannot endure harmonious tones but flee from them, because they are now repugnant. This is how David, by his harp playing, expelled the evil spirit from Saul. . . . Thus music and song were introduced into divine service by the [Hebrew] prophets and the [Church] fathers, who were well versed in the mysteries of harmony.*

At this point it is apposite to mention that, according to Dr. Franz HARTMANN (1838–1912), Dr. Carl D. ISENBERG (1876–1941), and Dr. Carl WICKLAND (1862–1837) among others, non-organic mental illnesses are due to the sufferer being possessed (Latin: *possessio*) by evil spirits.[27]

Incidentally, according to the Kabbalist R. ABENEZRA (Abraham ibn Esra ben Meir (1090–1164), "the Biblical healing of Saul by the harping of David is believed to have taken place because David knew the stars by which the music had to be regulated in order to effect a cure."[28] Terpander (Terpandros) was a lyric poet of Ancient Greece, a native of Antissa on the island of Lesbos who lived mostly in Sparta. He flourished at the end of the seventh century B.C.

THE MUSIC OF INANIMATE NATURE
(Chapter XXIV)

> *But there is something even more amazing. On the Attic shore, the sea itself sounds like a lyre.*

I set this down without doubting its general truthfulness; for Dr. STEGE (died in 1967) has supplied us with enough examples[29] of how and where wind, water, and sand make music together. One of his instances is the "singing" Röderbachtal [Röder brook dale] near Thronecken,[30] or Drohnecken (Hunsrück).

---

[27] Carl Wickland, *Dreissig Jahre unter den Toten* [Thirty Years Among the Dead], Remagen, 1957.

[28] Stege, 145.

[29] Dr. Fritz Stege, *Musik—Magie—Mystik* [Music—Magic—Mysticism], Remagen, 1961, 49.

[30] Stege, 49–50.

SINGING STONES
(Chapter XXIV)

In Megara there is a stone that, every time it is struck, sounds like a lyre being played.

"Alexander von HUMBOLDT (1769–1859) reported the existence of tinkling rocks on the banks of the Orinoco."[31] Dr. STEGE made a survey of how the tonal characteristics of certain types of stone has been interpreted musically.[32]

MUSICAL SECRETS OF NATURE
(Chapter XLI)

Claudian sang concerning it: "There is a place on the furthest coast of Gaul where are heard the whispering laments and faint sounds of floating shades. . . ." Aristotle relates that there used to be a tumulus on Lipara, one of the Aeolian islands near Italy, which it was dangerous to visit at night; the sound of cymbals and castanets was said to have been heard there together with uncanny laughter; also those who lived nearby declared that one could hear noises of all sorts and weird music. . . . In Norway there is an extremely horrible mountain encircled by the sea, popularly known as Hechelberg and having a hellish aspect, where such a doleful howling and screaming is made that the ghastly din is audible from a mile away. . . . What is more, there is a mountain in Scotland, and one in Thuringia, where frightful wailings are heard. . . . Again, there are similar prodigies in various countries and regions; and what I myself have seen with my own eyes and touched with my own hands I will not record here, in case I am branded a liar, on account of their astounding nature, by sceptical folk.

---

[31] Dr. Fritz Stege, *Musik—Magie—Mystik* [Music—Magic—Mysticism], Remagen, 1961, 49.
[32] Stege, 49–50.

Modern examples are the singing rocks of the Orinoco, a "spirit grotto" in the Sri Lankan jungle, the singing Röderbachtal near Thronecken or Drohnecken (Hunsrück), and the subterranean concert performed by the rocks in Norway.[33] CLAUDIAN of Alexandria was one of the last exponents of Latin poetry in the fourth century and was court poet to the first Western emperor, Flavius Honorius (395–423).

KEPLER'S HARMONY OF THE COSMOS
(Chapter XXVI)

Some also derive the harmony of the heavenly bodies from their respective distances. Thus the distance of the Moon from Earth is one hundred and twenty-six thousand Italian stadia, which is the interval of a tone; from the Moon to Mercury the distance is only half as great, which makes a semitone; another semitone is formed by the distance from Venus to Mercury. The three-and-a-half times longer distance between Earth and the Sun (including the one-and-a-half distance between Venus and the Sun) makes a fifth. The two-and-a-half times longer distance to the Sun from the Moon makes a fourth; so from the Sun to Mars the distance is the same as from Earth to the Moon, or a tone; the half-as-great distance to Jupiter from Mars is another semitone, and from Jupiter to Saturn is also a semitone; and between Saturn and the starry heaven is the space of a semitone. . . . Therefore the distance to the Sun from the starry heaven is a fourth, or two-and-a-half tones, and that to Earth from the starry heaven is an octave, or six whole tones.

Dr. STEGE draws attention to a similar notion in the *Harmonice mundi* of 1619[34] written by Johannes KEPLER (1571–1630): "The actual distance of the inferior planets (Mercury, Venus, Earth) from the Sun amounts to 58, 108 and 149 million kilometers,

[33] Dr. Fritz Stege, *Musik—Magie—Mystik* [Music—Magic—Mysticism], Remagen, 1961, 49 f.

[34] Johannes Kepler, *Harmonice mundi* (Ausg. o. J. Bryk), Jena, 1918.

which is nearly in the ratio of 1 : 2 : 3, or fundamental tone, octave, and fifth. That the present distances should be eternally fixed is unthinkable: might not these ratios have been a "pure" 50 : 100 : 150 at one time?"[35]

For further information the reader is referred to the useful little reference book, *Die Aspekt-Lehre nach Johannes Kepler* [Johannes Kepler's Theory of the (Astrological) Aspects] by Dr. Walter KOCH (born in 1895), which was issued as a reprint in 1952 by the "Astrologische Studienhefte," Hamburg [See also, J. V. Field, *Kepler's Geometrical Cosmology*, Athlone Press, London, 1988. Tr.]. In this connection we must not forget the so-called BODE-TITIUS law of planetary distances. "It was discovered in 1766 by the Wittenberg professor, TITIUS (1729–1796) and was later confirmed and popularized by Johann Elert BODE (1747–1826). It has the formula:

$$A = a + b^{\pi}b \ (a = 0.4; b = 0.3)$$

which gives the distances A of the planets . . . in astronomical units when π successively takes the values -00, 0, 1, 2, 4, 5, 6. The omission π = 3 is supplied by the average distance of the asteroids."[36] Perhaps the formula will be easier to understand if the distance from Earth to the Sun is made equal to 10. If this is done, the distances of

Mercury	=	4	Jupiter	=	52
Venus	=	7	Saturn	=	100
Earth	=	10	Uranus	=	196
Mars	=	16	Neptune	=	388

On subtracting 4 from these numbers, we obtain:

Mercury	=	0	Jupiter	=	48
Venus	=	3	Saturn	=	96
Earth	=	6	Uranus	=	192
Mars	=	12	Neptune	=	384
[Asteroids]	=	24			

The number 24 is where the asteroids come. On the basis of the above series, it was guessed that some planet ought to occur at this

---

[35] Dr. Fritz Stege, *Musik—Magie—Mystik* [Music—Magic—Mysticism], Remagen, 1961, 12.

[36] Prof. Karl Stumpff, *Astronomie* [Astronomy] ("das Fischer Lexicon"), data supplied by Schrödter, Frankfurt/M., 1957, 223–224.

orbital distance, and one of its fragments, the asteroid Ceres, which helped to fill the gap, "was discovered on January 1, 1801 by Giuseppe PIAZZI (1746–1826) as he scanned the sky at Palermo."[37]

THE HUMAN PENTAGRAM
(Chapter XXVII)

If, from this midpoint, a circle is described so as to pass over the crown of the head, and if the arms are lowered until the fingertips touch the circumference of this circle, and the feet are spread apart at the same distance as the fingertips are separated from the crown of the head, the circle will be divided into five equal arcs, and a perfect pentagram will be constructed; also the two heels and the navel will form an equilateral triangle.

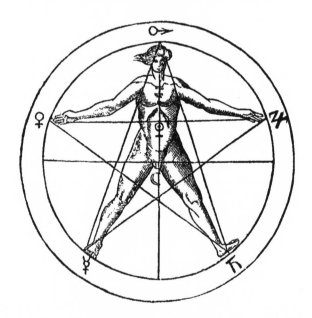

Hewn ten feet above the giant altar stone in the rock cathedral at Montségur (3937 ft.) in the French Pyrenees, is a five-pointed figure in which a person stood in the pentagram position during

---

[37] Ibid.

Cathar ceremonies. The pentagram, or five-pointed star, is the diagrammatic representation of the human being. "Apart from its other meanings," says Manfred KYBER (1880–1933), "this figure corresponds to the pose of someone with outstretched arms and legs in the form of a pentagram, and in general to the purely vegetative powers of the body. Just try resting in this position when you are completely exhausted, and you will find that you regain strength much more quickly than in any other position."[38] PARACELSUS regarded the pentagram as the most effective character or sigil in magical work (*Philosophia occulta*, vol. IX).

MOTHER SUN
(Chapter XXXII)

Iamblichus says that whatever good we possess we have obtained from the Sun either directly or indirectly . . . and many Platonists have identified the Sun as the seat of the World Soul; in their opinion it [the Sun] is fully imbued with the latter, so that its beams (so to speak) pour something spiritual into the All, and transmit life, feeling, and activity to the universe as a whole. Therefore the old natural philosophers called the Sun the heart of the universe. . . . The Sun is singled out from the other stars as an image of the great Lord of the two worlds, the earthly and the heavenly, the true light and the most faithful representative of God . . . so that the [Platonic] Academicians have nothing clearer with which to express the being of God. . . . It stands in such an inner relationship to God that Plato terms it the visible Son of God.

It is striking how a noted biologist and metabiologist of our own times—Dr. Herbert FRITSCHE (1911–1960)—says exactly the same thing as our old friend Agrippa, "only in slightly different words": "If sunlight is full of that organic energy by which vegetable nutriment is synthesized and rendered organ-

---

[38] Manfred Kyber, *Einführung i. d. Gesamtgebiet Okkultismus vom Altertum bis zur Gegenwart* [An Introduction to the Whole Field of Occultism from Ancient Times to the Present Day], Stuttgart, 1923, 23.

ic, then the Sun must be more than an astrophysical object. The physical activities of the Sun are relatively minor; its systematizing power extends beyond the realm of matter. And even so, the Sun's being cannot be exhausted by these activities. In his last conversation with ECKERMANN, GOETHE declared that it was natural for him to pay devout reverence to JESUS, and that it was also in his nature to venerate the Sun, 'for it is likewise a revelation of the Highest, and indeed it is the mightiest that is granted to us children of earth to behold'"[39] We may recall that Jesus Himself said, "I am the light of the world."[40]

THE MOON AND ITS MAGICAL ASSOCIATIONS
(Chapter XXXII)

As Earth's neighbor, the Moon is the container of the celestial influences. . . . Thus it exercises on the things here below an influence that is far more obvious than that of anything else, and its activity is perceptible because of its proximity and because of the inner relationship it has with us, since it is the intermediary between the Superior and the Inferior. And so the course of the Moon ought to be observed first of all. . . . Therefore we would be unable to draw down the power from above without the interposition of the Moon, so that Thebit prescribes that in order to obtain the power of any star one must take a stone, and likewise a plant, ruled by that star, either when the Moon passes under that star in a fortunate hour or makes an easy aspect to it.

The importance of the Moon in "sympathetic cures," in plant and animal breeding, and in biological processes, is an inexhaustible topic.[41]

---

[39] Herbert Fritsche, *Der Erstgeborene: Ein Bild des Menschen* [The Firstborn: An Image of Mankind], Berlin, 1940, 22.

[40] John VIII: 12.

[41] Willy Schrödter, *Grenz. Vers.* [Paranormal Research for All], 149 f., chapter on "The Moon." "The Influence of the Moon on Terrestrial Things" in *Okk. Stimme,* Parts 29, 30/IV; 5, 6/V, Brunswick 1953, 1954; and "Seltsame Wirkungen des Mondlichts" [Peculiar Effects of Moonlight] in *Die Andere Welt,* Part 4, Freiburg, April, 1962, 219 f.

THE GOLDEN CHAIN
(Chapter XXXII)

²Also, there commences with the Moon the series that Plato calls "the Golden Chain," in which each thing depends on the thing above it by a linkage of causation, until we reach the highest cause of all on which all things depend.

On the evening of December 7, 1768, Johann Wolfgang von GOETHE was quickly and permanently cured of his deadly and baffling Leipzig disease in Frankfurt/Main by the alchemical physician Dr. Johann Friedrich METZ (1724–1782), who used a mysterious "universal medicine"[42] in the form of "a salt." The prince of poets gave a detailed account of the incident in *Dichtung und Wahrheit* [Fact and Fiction] (II; 8), and he applied himself to alchemical-kabbalistic studies after his recovery.[43] In the main, he concentrated on the *Aurea Catena Homeri,* an advanced Rosicrucian textbook published in 1723, and reissued in 1781 as *Annulus Platonis,* the author of which was the fundamental researcher Dr. Anton Joseph KIRCHWEGER (died 1746).[44]

When Faust first sees the sign of the Macrocosm, GOETHE makes him exclaim concerning the interconnection of things:

---

[42] Willy Schrödter, "Gedanken zur Hindu-Medizin und zu analogen Methoden der abendländischen Medizin" [Reflections on Hindu Medicine and on Analogous Methods of Western Medicine] in *Erfahrungsheilkunde,* Parts 4, 5, 6, Ulm/Donau, April/May/June, 1958, 184 f., 224, 274 f.

[43] Willy Schrödter, *Geschichte und Lehren der Rosenkreuzer* [History and Doctrines of the Rosicrucians], Villach, 1956, 64.

[44] Ferd. Maack, *Die goldene Kette Homers,* Lorch/W. Goethe describes how Faust sees the sign of the Macrocosm on opening a "Book of Mystery from Nostradamus' very hand"—as Bayard Taylor (1825–1878) renders it in his translation of *Faust* (New York, n.d., 13). However, Taylor takes issue with Goethe on this point and has a note to the effect that the words read by Faust in the "Book of Mystery" just before he expresses wonder at the Sign of the Microcosm "are not from Nostradamus. They may possibly have been suggested by something in Jacob Boehme's first work, *Aurora.*" (Bayard Taylor, *Goethe's Faust,* p. 168). Be that as it may, Willy Schrödter is probably correct in pointing us in the direction of the *Aurea Catena Homeri* because that book commences with a diagram showing a descending chain of circular (or link-like) alchemical signs. The topmost link is labeled "confused chaos," and the chain descends through the chemical, animal, vegetable, and mineral kingdoms to the "unfermented root" and the Philosopher's Stone. Tr.

See how all are intertwined into a whole—
    With each one living and working in the other!
See how the heavenly powers ascend and descend
    And share the contents of their golden urns!
With blessèd odors winging
    From Heaven down to Earth
All sound harmoniously through the All![45]

Since it has something in common with the present topic, we may think of another "golden chain" here, which is "spiritual" rather than "elementary," and is referred to by the adept Eugenius PHILALETHES (Thomas Vaughan, born in 1622) as "Jacob's Ladder" (cf. Genesis XXVII: 10 f.). "Jacob's ladder is the greatest mystery in the Kabbalah. Here we find two extremes: Jacob is one at the foot of the ladder and God is the other Who stands above it, shedding some secret influx of spirit upon Jacob, who in this place typifies the human being in general. The rounds or steps in the ladder signify the middle nature by which Jacob is united to God, inferiors united to superiors."[46]

This spiritual hierarchy is mentioned by Johann Christoph Friedrich von SCHILLER (1759–1805) in his "Die Piccolomini" (1798, II: 6) as follows:

That which weaves mysterious meaning
    And builds in nature's depths—
The spiritual ladder that from the world of dust,
    And with a thousand rungs,
Rises to the starry world.
    The heavenly powers upon it
Travel up and down.
    Its circles within circles, drawing
Closer round the central Sun,
    Are visible to unsealed eyes alone;
Eyes of the light-born, joyous
    Children of Jove.

---

[45] J. W. v. Goethe, *Faust* (Lines 447–453 in the Reclam edition), Stuttgart, 1948, 17.
[46] (Eugenius Philalethes, *Magia Adamica; Coelum terrae,* 1650). A. E. Waite, ed., *The Works of Thomas Vaughan.* Theosophical Publishing House, London, 1919, 169–170.

THE WORLD SOUL AND THE SOUL OF THE HEAVENLY BODIES
(Chapter LV)

Since the heavens and the heavenly bodies have a powerful influence and an unmistakable effect on the things of our world, they must necessarily possess souls, because an effect of that sort cannot be exercised by a mere body. And so the celebrated poets and philosophers have maintained that both the universe and the heavenly bodies possess a soul, and that this soul is rational.

This statement is then supported by quotations. In chapter LVII, AGRIPPA endeavors to show that the World Soul and also the souls of the heavenly bodies are rational and share the divine powers of understanding. Among other things, he writes:

In addition it would be extremely foolish to believe that the heavenly souls and the soul of the universe act blindly . . . since the perfection of the body is the soul, and the more perfect a body is, the more perfect the soul is that occupies it. Therefore the heavenly bodies, being the most perfect, must necessarily have the most perfect souls.

The concept of the ensoulment of the heavenly bodies can be traced from PLATO (427–347) in his *Philebus* through Johannes KEPLER (1571-1630) in his *Harmonice mundi* (1619), Gustav Theodor FECHNER (1801–1887), Prof. Maximilian PERTY (1804–1884) with his *Geodämon,* and Max VALIER (1895–1930) with his "occult doctrine of the universe,"[47] to name but a few. [48] Without a belief in the ensoulment of the stars, the idea that it is possible to invoke them (the star gods and planetary rulers) would never have arisen. In chapter XXXVI of Book Three, we read that "the world is a rational, immortal creation." What is more, in today's ecological and anthroposophical circles it is agreed that "the earth is a living organism." ["Gaia." Tr.].

---

[47] Surya-Valier, *Okkulte Weltallslehre* [An Occult Doctrine of the Universe], Munich, 1922.
[48] Willy Schrödter, *Astral-Mystik* [Astral Mysticism], 12 f.

THIRD BOOK

ON CEREMONIAL MAGIC

To work through the hidden forces of nature is natural magic; to work through the force behind all forces is divine magic; this is the highest wisdom, an approach to God, saintliness.

—Carl von ECKARTSHAUSEN (1752–1803)
Aufschlüsse zur Magie aus geprüften Erfahrungen, etc.
[Elucidation of Magic by Validated Experience]
Munich, 1792; Part IV; heading

The one magic is for the common people and always grovels on the ground; it has to do with ghosts and involves itself with dead bodies. But the other, concerning which we have enquired of priests and prophets from our youth, looks up to heaven, deals with the gods, and partakes of the essence of mighty beings.

—HELIODORUS (ca. 250)
Aithiopika (L.III)

There is a power of the soul that is elevated above all the powers of nature, and places us in a position to override all systems and all spheres of nature, and to participate actively in the immortal life and energy of the exalted heavenly beings. When the soul is totally raised to the beings that are superior to itself, it becomes completely segregated from lower natures and exchanges this life for another; quitting the order of things with which it has so far been bound up in order to be bound up and fused with another and higher one.

IAMBLICHUS (283–333)

FIRE MAGIC
(Chapter XI)

According to Pausanius, the Lydians had two temples, in the cities of Hierocaesarea and Hypepa, of the goddess they called Persica. Now whenever divine worship had to be celebrated in one of these temples, a magus laid dry wood on the altar and sang hymns in his native language, and then read aloud some barbarous words from a book he held in his hand. Scarcely had these been pronounced when the wood began to catch fire of its own accord without being lit, and burst into a very bright flame.

It may be recalled how Elijah (850 B.C.) built an altar on Mount Carmel (Hebrew for "vineyard," 1732 ft.) dug a trench round it, piled wood on it, and soaked it three times with water so thoroughly that the ditch almost overflowed. Then he called upon Yahweh and "the fire of the LORD fell, and consumed the burnt sacrifice, and the wood, and the stones, and the dust, and licked up the water that was in the trench." (I Kings XVIII: 38).

"In the ceremony of the *Kushandika Homa* the recitation of the appropriate mantra can kindle a fire without physical means."[1] For the truth of this assertion, we depend on the guarantee of the currently well-known and highly regarded alchemist and healer Max RETSCHLAG (Leipzig), supported by the equally distinguished Prague mystic Karl WEINFURTER (1870-1942), who declared, "not long ago, in the house of one of my friends, a person ignited some fuel without the aid of fire or matches by reciting a simple mantra, the so-called 'fire seed' (the syllable 'ram')."[2]

Sheikh Abdul VEHAB of Istanbul, who ran a bureau for psychic consultations and occult experiments in the 1920's, once entered a place of spiritual retreat (Tekké). However his thoughts kept wandering to his books. Suddenly he uttered an imprecation: "To hell with the lot of them!" And he informs us that "it was later confirmed that in that very hour a fire broke out

---

[1] Max Retschlag, *Die Alchimie und ihr gr. Meisterwerk* [Alchemy and its Great Work], Leipzig, 1934, 36.
[2] Karl Weinfurter, *Der brennende Busch* [The Burning Bush], Lorch/W., 1930, 137.

at my home in Pankaldi."[3] Franz BUCHMANN ("Naga") found
that "through experiments with a certain (fire) talisman real
lightning fell no more than three feet away in front of my associate."[4] Buchmann lived in Charlottenburg, his co-experimenter,
the mesmerist Heinrich HOFFMANN, lived in Auerbach a.d.
Bergstraße.

HEALING THE POSSESSED
(Chapter XII)

*Certainly Christ would not have said to His disciples:
they shall cast out devils in my name, etc., if authority
did not reside in his name over demons, diseases, serpents, poisons, speaking in tongues, and so on; an authority that comes both from the power of God and
from the power of Him who is called by this name, as
well as finally because of the power inherent in the
word JESUS itself. . . . Hence because each creature
fears and honors the name of the one who has created it,
occasionally even evil and impure people, provided
they believe in the invocation of this divine name, com-
pel demons and accomplish other great things.*

In chapter XXXII this theme reappears:

*Origen in his polemic "Against Celsus" alleges that
naming the name of JESUS is reputed to have often
expelled countless demons from the souls and bodies of
men and women.*

---

[3] Carl Vett, *Seltsame Erlebnisse in einem Derwischkloster* [Strange Experiences in a Dervish Monastery], Straßburg, 1931, 19–20.
[4] Franz Buchmann, *Schlüssel zu den 72 Gottesnamen der Kabbala* [A Key to the 72 Divine Names of the Kabbalah], Leipzig, 1925, 26. [These names are also listed by Johann Reuchlin in his *De Arte Cabalistica*, 1517. See *On the Art of the Kabbalah*, tr. Martin and Sarah Goodman, University of Nebraska Press, 1993, 273; see also: Papus, *The Qabalah*, Thorsons, Wellingborough, 1977, 266–291. Tr.]; Willy Schrödter, "Über die okkulte Natur der Kugelblitze" [The Occult Nature of Ball-Lightning] in *Die Andere Welt*, Parts 11 and 12, Freiburg, Nov./Dec., 1961, 686 f., 752 f.

Origen (185–255) is a celebrated Alexandrian Church Father who attempted to combine Christian theology and neoplatonic philosophy, and consequently had his teachings condemned as heretical. CELSUS—not to be confused with the physician of the same name!—lived in Rome as a Platonic philosopher in the second century and was well-known for his attacks on Christianity. It was for him that the *Lutherus medicorum* ["Luther of Medicine" i.e., iconoclastic medical reformer] Philipp von HOHENHEIM styled himself "Para-Celsus" i.e., "against Celsus" or "superior to Celsus."

The belief that many mental illnesses are due to possession by evil spirits is as old as the human race and is spread all over the world. As already mentioned, it is a view also shared by many modern physicians; to name but a few: Dr. Franz HARTMANN (1838–1912), Dr. Carl ISENBERG (1876–1941), Dr. Carl WICKLAND (1862–1937), and Dr. Titus BULL (1932). The Roman Catholic Church includes the healing of the possessed in the name of JESUS as a rite of exorcism in her *Rituale Romanum* and specifies certain characteristics that enable one to distinguish between a *possessio* and a nervous disorder. Those of the saints who have healed the possessed include St. Leonard and St. Zeno.

The Catholic priest Johann Josef GASSNER (1727–1779) healed tens of thousands of sufferers by casting out demons, first in Vorarlberg and then in Bavaria. The Evangelical pastor Johann Christoph BLUMHARDT (1805–1880) was similarly occupied in Möttlingen and then in Bad Boll.

EGREGORS
(Chapter LXX)

The terrestrial angels are in charge of public affairs, princes and magistrates, provinces and kingdoms, and each one has a special responsibility. Thus we read in the Book of Daniel: "The prince of the kingdom of Persia withstood me for twenty-one days; and behold [the angel] Michael, one of the chief [angel] princes came to help me; and I held my own against the kings of

Persia." . . . *Jesus the son of Sirach states that each nation has an angel set over it as its leader, which MOSES in his song in the fifth book [of the Torah] seems to suggest when he says: "When the Lord divided the nations, he set their borders according to the number of the angels of God" (Deuteronomy 32: 8).*

The Kabbalah names 72 such national angelic regents,[5] which the Hebrews call Elohim; the metaphysical technical term Egregors is also used for them. Derived from the Greek word *egregoros,* it means "watcher" or "guardian."

The office of a Watcher is to protect from outside pressures a region or ethnic group assigned to its care. The region is always measured off from another posing a threat of some sort to it. A given group of persons (the group of those who are being protected) is "tied" to a certain area of jurisdiction. This is where the "stereosophic mystery of magical seclusion" comes in, to borrow the language of the Hamburg stereosoph, allomatic, and Rosicrucian researcher, Dr. Ferdinand MAACK (1861–1930).[6] Here, too, we meet the "riddle of the founding of cities and states" which has occupied thinkers from HERODOTUS (-500 B.C.) and PLATO (Aristokles, 427–347 B.C.) through Nobel prize winner and member of the Académie Française, Anatole FRANCE (Jacques-François Thibaut, 1844–1924).[7]

What is more, both the ancient Romans,[8] and until quite recently the Chinese,[9] have recognized the existence of guardian spirits set over cities. Indeed, one author reports as follows on the occult war waged on enemy cities by ancient Rome: "The Romans, when besieging a city, made a habit of carefully enquiring the name of the city and of its guardian spirit. When they knew

[5] Franz Buchmann ("Naga"), *Schlüssel z. d. 72 Gottesnamen der Kabbala* [A Key to the 72 Divine Names of the Kabbalah], Leipzig, 1919; Sersheim i. Wttbg., ca. 1955; and Papus, *The Qabalah,* Thorsons, Wellingborough, 1977, 266–291.

[6] Willy Schrödter, "Von den Egregoren" [Article on Egregors] in *Natur und Kultur,* Series 4, Munich-Solln, October, 1955, 234–236; "Egregor Chinas" [The Egregor of China] in *Geister/Mystik/Magie,* Berlin W 30, 1958, 137–145; Ferd. Maack, *Heilge Mathesis* [Sacred Numerology], Leipzig, 1924, 42 f.

[7] Anatole France, *La Rôtisserie de la Reine Pédauque,* Paris, 1893.

[8] Agrippa, Book III, ch. 14.

[9] Werner Eichhorn, *China gestern / heute / morgen* [China Yesterday, Today and Tomorrow], Leipzig, 1929, 141.

these, they would summon the guardian spirit of the city by means of a spell, and would execrate the city and its inhabitants, and conquer it."[10] The words of the curse are known to me and I have supplied them elsewhere.[11]

"A similar operation, but in a more circumscribed area, is reported by the Jewish historian Flavius JOSEPHUS (37–100) in his *The Jewish War*. The Church History of the Greek Church Father, EUSEBIUS of Caesarea (264–339) retells this event from Josephus. The story goes that, when in the year 70, Jerusalem was about to fall to Flavius Vespasianus Titus (39–81) by whom it was being besieged, a great uproar was heard in the temple. The voice of an invisible being—that of the archangel Michael—commanded the host of angels gathered there to leave the temple; they withdrew from the holy place and from the doomed city with a fearful roar. According to the traditional belief concerning angels—people, houses, cities, and nations perish when they are abandoned by their indwelling angels."[12]

GUARDIAN ANGELS
(Chapter XX)

Those individuals to whom the higher angels are allotted gain preference, because their guardian angels elevate them and cause others to become subject to them by means of a certain occult force. Although neither party understands what is happening, the inferior person feels himself to be under a yoke that is not easily thrown off; indeed, he has a profound nervousness of this force exercised by the superior on the inferior. . . . Thus we read of Mark Antony, that he had once been a

---

[10] Agrippa, Book I, ch. 70; Prof. Angelo Brelich, *Die geheime Schutzgottheit von Rom* [The Secret Tutelary God of Rome].

[11] Willy Schrödter, "Metaphysische Kampfesweise" [Metaphysical Methods of Warfare] in *Interne Mitteilungen der Ges. f. wiss. Spiritismus e. V.,* Circular 29, Hannover, April, 1953, 320–322.

[12] Alfons ROSENBERG, "Flugblätter für Freunde a. d. Werkstatt von Alfons ROSEN-BERG" [Pamphlets for Friends Attending Alfons Rosenberg's Workshop]; Horw-Luzern, 32nd pamphlet, Whitsun, 1965, "The Secret of the Jewish People," extract: "The Angel and the Times," p. 2, data supplied by W. Schrödter.

close friend of Octavianus Augustus and had often
played with him; but since Augustus was always the
winner, a magus is said to have uttered the following
warning to Mark Antony: "What have you to do, O
Antony, with yonder youth! Flee from and avoid him!
For although you are older in years and richer in expe-
rience, and are of nobler birth and have been successful
as a general in many battles, nevertheless your genius
fears the genius of your youth, your luck smiles at him
and seems—if you do not flee—to want to desert to
him completely." ... *Is not a prince a man like any oth-*
er? So how would the others stand in such awe of him,
if divine dignity did not raise him up and fill them
with such respect that they honored him as their
prince? Therefore we must try, by being purified
through virtuous behavior and striving after higher
things, to receive higher and mightier angels, and be-
come entitled to take precedence over others.

SHAKESPEARE takes this theme up in his tragedy "Antony and
Cleopatra" (Act II; Scene 3).

The soothsayer to Antony:

Thy demon—that's thy spirit which keeps thee—is
Noble, courageous, high, unmatchable,
Where Caesar is not; but near him thy angel
Becomes a fear, as being o'erpowered; therefore
Make space enough between you . . .
If thou dost play with him at any game
Thou art sure to lose, and, of that natural luck,
He beats thee 'gainst the odds; thy lustre thickens
When he shines by. I say again, thy spirit
Is all afraid to govern thee near him.
But he away, 'tis noble.

Antony then says to himself:

He hath spoken true; the very dice obey him,
And in our sports my better cunning faints
Under his chance; if we draw lots he speeds.

Also in "Macbeth" (Act III, Scene 1), Shakespeare puts the following soliloquy into the mouth of this king of Scotland (1040–1057):

My genius is rebuked, as it is said
Mark Antony's was by Caesar.

And the frequently mentioned CARUS had something to say on the subject.[13] There is also Schiller's insight concerning Goethe, which he confided to Christian Gottfried Körner on March 9, 1789: "This individual, this Goethe, obstructs me greatly, and he reminds me so often that fate has not treated me well. How effortlessly is his genius buoyed up by his fate, and how must I keep struggling to this very hour."[14]

It should be mentioned for the record that the well-known English spiritist, William Thomas STEAD (1849–1912) is said, while witnessing the coronation of the British king, to have perceived clairvoyantly how exalted angelic beings descended during the ceremony and how a change took place in the king's aura the moment he was anointed, because the divine forces poured into his body and raised him above other men and women (in keeping with the theory of the "divine right of kings"!).[15]

HOW ANGELS AND SPIRITS SPEAK
(Chapter XXIII)

As everyone knows, in order to speak, we need our tongues and the other speech organs, namely teeth, throat, lungs, windpipe, and chest muscles, which are activated by the soul. If anyone wishes to say something to someone in the distance, he has to raise

---

[13] Carus, 224.
[14] Emil Staiger, *Der Briefwechsel zwischen Schiller und Goethe* [The Letters of Schiller and Goethe], Frankfurt, 1966.
[15] Ludwig Deinhard, *Die englische Krönungsfeier vom Standpunkt des Okkulten* [The English Coronation from the Standpoint of the Occultist], in *Ztrbl. f. Okkultismus*, Part 2 Leipzig, August, 1911, 102–111.

his voice, whereas he can whisper in the ear of the person next to him; and, if the breath containing his words could be united even more closely with the listener, his speech would no longer have to make a sound but would flow into the listener noiselessly, just as a picture falls on the eye and on a mirror. This is how souls that have been separated from their bodies, and angels, and demons, speak, and what human beings do audibly, these do inaudibly by impressing on the listener merely the sense of what they are saying, and they do it more perfectly than if the listener could hear them. . . . The fact is that the spirit body of demons is entirely and universally so rarefied that it touches, sees, and hears without a medium and nothing can obstruct it. . . . Yet the spirits do not perceive with spiritual organs constructed on the same plan as our physical organs; it is more likely that they absorb with their whole bodies, like sponges, everything that is perceptible, or receive impressions in some unknown way. In any case, even animals do not all have the same sense organs; for, as we know, many are without ears and yet hear sounds, although we do not know how they do it.

If we may comment briefly on the fine example of the all-absorbing sponge surrounded by water, which is used in the above extract to illustrate the "universal sense," the merging of at least two senses, hearing and sight, was known to the Ancient Chinese and was aptly termed "ear light."[16] The French mystic Jeanne Marie Bouvier de La Motte GUYON (1648–1717) has this to say in her autobiography concerning her relationship with her father confessor: "When the (Barnabite) father Peter LACOMBE was admitted to hear my confession or give me communion, I was unable to converse with him without the same silence arising within me as in the presence of God. I think God wished to teach me that even in this life people can understand the language of angels. Gradually I reached the

---

[16] Stege, 97; Marius Schneider, *Singende Steine* [Singing Stones], Kassel-Wilhelmshöhe, 1958, 10.

stage where I could converse with the father in utter silence. And so we understood one another in God in an inexpressible and divine manner. We spent hours in this deep silence constantly gathering one another's thoughts without having to say a word."[17]

WEATHER MAGIC
(Chapter XXIV)

I have seen someone writing the name and seal of a spirit on virgin parchment in the hour of the Moon and, after giving the parchment to a frog to eat and muttering a spell, allowing the frog to jump into the water; and I have seen how this has soon been followed by heavy rain. . . . The same person wrote, in my presence, the name of another spirit together with its seal in the hour of Mars and gave the writing to a raven, which he released after muttering a spell; whereupon from the same part of the sky toward which the raven flew there arrived a severe electric storm, with vivid lightning and terrible claps of thunder.

Our author witnessed this performance on two occasions, and on each occasion animals were the vehicles employed. If we accept that, whenever the mage employed an animal, it just did him the favor of eating or making off with his writing, then we have to assume that it acted under some compelling influence. This is quite apart from the question of whether or not it is possible for someone using a sigil to prevail upon a spirit being to change the weather the way they want it. Now the art of weather control is not only (usually in a bad sense) attributed to witches and claimed by them, so that even today in Rhenish Hessia the term "weather witch" is applied to any headstrong female, but reputable folk will vouch for the truth of it. For example, the Hamburg hermeticist, Alfred MÜLLER-EDLER (1875–1960) wrote to me as follows on December 7, 1947:

---

[17] Eira Hellberg, *Telepathie: Okkulte Kräfte,* Prien/Obbay, 1922, 56 f; Schrödter, *Präsenzwirkung,* 53 f.

I knew a man in Altona called Julius K., who was proficient in this art. He created a violent electric storm, which he released over Groß-Borstel. On one occasion he presented me with a magic seal he had made and invited me to use it. I could not screw up the courage to do so, and I burned the uncanny thing. . . . When I was with him indoors, the heavy pendulums (weighing approximately two pounds) behaved so wildly that it often thundered between them, and the spirits had to be told to be quiet.[18]

In one of my books I referred to a "thief-charmer" of the Kaufunger forest near Cassel; whereupon a lay healer living in Cassel wrote to me on August 25, 1960 (quite recently therefore!) that the person concerned did not live in the Kaufungerwald but in the Habichtswald—and that on one occasion the man had whipped up a storm within ten minutes before his very eyes![19]

Here is another modern example: in 1959 a news item was carried by the popular press, including the *Freiburger Zeitung,* and should be easy to verify: "Gunner John A. GOODWILL of the Canadian artillery regiment stationed in Derlinghofen near Hemer is a genuine Sioux chief from Fort Qu'Appelle in the Canadian prairie province of Saskatchewan. During the recent heatwave in Northern Germany—Goodwill's regiment was on maneuvers on the Lüneburg Heath, and the exercises were going to be abandoned due to the risk of fire—the uniformed Indian chief prayed for rain by the traditional "rainmaker's dance" of his tribe. After half an hour of mystic body movements, gesticulations, and invocations, the first drops of rain began to fall. He observed to his astonished comrades, "I have done nothing more than what my grandfather taught me."

All I can do is to take note of this and bring it to the reader's attention. I long ago gave up dismissing anything out of hand.

---

[18] Willy Schrödter, *Erlebnisse und Erzählungen eines Wissenden* [Experiences and Narrations of an Esoterist], in *Die andere Welt,* Part 12, Freiburg/Brsg, December, 1960, 556.
[19] Schrödter, *A Rosicrucian Notebook*, Weiser, 1992.

SEALS OF SPIRITS
(Chapter XXX)

Not that we could at all draw down spirits through characters, figures, and sigils, but that we ascend to them through these things by concentrating our internal and external senses on them, and then being seized by admiration we are inclined to a religious veneration of them and are caught up in an ecstasy of devotion to a state of wonderworking faith, certain hope, and animating love; and invoking them, with sincere minds, by their real names and characters, we obtain from them the power we desire.

Earlier in the same chapter, mention is made of monograms made by interweaving several letters. Our mage refers to them as follows:

This style is beloved of the Arabs, and there are no letters so easily and artistically combined as the Arabic.

This mention of arabesques, which Pierre Charles BAUDE-LAIRE (1821–1867) called "spiritual patterns," reveals deep insight. Arabesques or moresques are extremely intricate and fantastic convolutions in which Arabic letters are often included as a substratum.[20] What is more, the Bektashi dervishes form highly symbolic images from the Arabic letters.

---

[20] Ernst Kühnel, *Die Arabeske: Sinn und Wandlung eines Ornaments* [Arabesques: The Rationale and Transformation of an Ornamentation], Wiesbaden, 1949.

Now arabesques in general so strikingly resemble mediumistic ornamentation (produced in a state of trance) that one is bound to ask if, conversely, a state of trance is not capable of being induced in susceptible persons when they stare at moresques? Three experts agree with me in answering yes: "A state of suggestibility is induced by them (the arabesques), just as is also done by Arabic music and dance. . . . The oriental pattern diffuses our attention, and distracts us from everyday affairs and problems to a kind of self-hypnosis through which we can reach a metaphysical state of concentration, just as the Hindu enters a state of trance by prolonged gazing at his Yantra or ornamental tool of meditation.[21]

Former assistant schoolmaster, Hans HÄNIG, in an article on religious art in the Orient, written following a trip in the summer of 1927 to the Hagia Sofia and the Sultan Achmed mosque in Istanbul, says: "In both buildings the floor is covered by costly carpets displaying the most varied colors and well able to induce states of ecstasy. This may be compared with reports concerning people who, when under the influence of peyote see fantastic brightly-colored kaleidoscopic pictures pass before their eyes in quick succession. These are obviously the prototypes of those oriental carpet patterns that often seem so strange to Europeans and yet clearly come from the highest level of religious experience (compare also mediumistic dream paintings!)." When in such handwoven carpets, arabesques appear with outlines that are highly reminiscent of cloud banners,[22] we might not be wrong in thinking that this "cloudlike border" has some affinity with Tibetan lama exercises in which daily absorption in cloud formations leads to "formless ecstasy."[23]

Emmy WYSSLING (died 1967) reported when writing of her stay in Bosnia: "Oriental influences are certainly found in rural woven work and embroidery, with their distinctive geometrical patterns in which the design and its background are so evenly balanced that it is impossible to tell one from the other. By staring at them for a period the gazer can fall into a dreamy passivity.

---

[21] Ernst Diez, *Glaube und Welt des Islams* [The Faith and World of Islam], Stuttgart, 1941, 176 f.

[22] Kühnel, 23.

[23] Alexandra David-Neel, *Meister und Schüler* [Master and Pupil], Leipzig, 1934, 104.

These patterns are called *Zemân* [and] *Zemîn,* which means "space and time" in Arabic.[24] Thus spirit seals are ornamental devices for inducing trance states ("ornamental autohypnosis").

| Hebrew | Greek | Latin |

Monograms of the name of the archangel Michael.

INVOCATION OF SAINTS PREFERRED TO INVOCATION OF ANGELS
(Chapter XXXIV)

But we believe, regarding our holy heroes, that they are able to do great things by divine power; as the Hebrew theologians also testify, the spirit of the MESSIAH (i.e., JESUS CHRIST) rules over them all, and dispenses various gifts of His grace in the world below through different saints who are suitable vehicles for them, so that the saints have various offices. Therefore when we address them in prayer they most willingly bestow on us, according to the manifold distribution of the graces, their own special gifts, benefits, and favors and indeed they do so more quickly and even more abundantly than the angelic powers since they stand nearer to us and have more affinity with our nature, as they themselves were once human beings and experienced human sufferings and infirmities. What is more, their names, degrees, and functions are known to us.

---

[24] Emmy Wyssling, *Von Gebräuchen und Riten bei bosnischen Bauern* [Customs and Rites of the Bosnian Peasantry], from an unpublished manuscript and lecture given to the "Parapsychological Society," Zürich, 1960/61.

Not only does each profession have its patron saint, but even the various diseases are treated by particular saints. For example, St. Ottily is petitioned for eye diseases. G. W. SURYA (Demeter Georgiewicz-Weitzer, 1873–1949), the reviver of "occult medicine," wrote to me on one occasion that the same applies to many magnetic healers as applies to Catholic saints; invocations to given saints are recommended for given diseases, because they have a special power over them.

SOUL-GRAFTING
(Chapter XLI)

Also it is granted to the spirits of saintly individuals to dwell in us and illuminate us like good angels, as we read of how the spirit of Elijah (after he had been removed from the human world) came upon Elisha . . . .[25] *And in another place we read how God took some of the spirit that was in Moses and gave it to seventy men.*[26] *A great mystery lies hidden here, which may not be disclosed lightly.*

What is being referred to here is *Ibbûr* (Hebrew for "soul impregnation"), which Gustav MEYRINK (1868–1932) made the theme of chapter "J" of his best-seller *Der Golem* [The Golem]. Carl WELKISCH (born in 1888) called it "association,"[27] I term it "soul-grafting," and recently it has become known as "white possession" in agreement with the similar "black possession." Because of the importance of the subject, and the interest it will probably arouse, I shall offer at this point a couple of curious quotations. About a hundred years ago Fr. von MEYER wrote in his "Blättern für höhere Wahrheit" [Leaflets on Behalf of Higher Truth], (Set 9, p. 272):

---

[25] II Kings 2: 9, 10, 13–15.
[26] Numbers 11: 16–17, 24–25.
[27] Carl Welkisch, *Im Geistfeuer Gottes* [In God's Spiritual Fire], Remagen, 1957.

The rabbis, especially the Kabbalistic ones, maintain that the soul of someone who has died can have a secret influence on a living person, and can inspire him or even dwell in him and possess him, without the suppression of either personality, although these intermingle in thinking, willing, and doing. They even believe that several such souls can occupy an individual, just as demons do one possessed. They call this state of being indwelt by spirits Ibbûr, as if it were a sort of impregnation. We will not deny that it might be possible. What is more, an Ibbûr of some sort can occur between two living persons.

Now let us hear what a Kabbalist, the great Isaac LURIA (1534– 1572) has to say in his book on the transmigration of souls (Part I, chapter 5): "Soul impregnation (Ibbûr) occurs when a soul enters the body of someone who is already born and has reached maturity. When another soul enters such a person, the latter is, in a way, like someone carrying a baby inside her—hence the term 'soul impregnation.' As already said, this happens only in an adult, that is one who is at least 13 years and one day old, because from that age he is an adult and obliged to keep all the religious requirements. Therefore only then does that other soul enter him in order to help him and make him a righteous man by urging him to obey all the commandments of the Holy Law. This soul impregnation takes place on two accounts: firstly if the incoming soul had been unable to perform a duty that was not of such a nature that it was compelled to undergo a further metempsychosis (Gilgûl), and therefore it enters the man simply for another opportunity to fulfil the obligation. Or, secondly, if that soul is visiting the soul already present, because the owner of the latter needs the help of the additional soul to make him righteous and to guide him. For the newly arrived soul is faultless. In either case, the soul impregnation does not occur before the age of 13 years and one day. What is more, there is the following difference between the two cases: when the impregnating soul joins the original one in order to make good its own deficiencies, it diffuses itself, like the host's own soul, throughout his whole body, it suffers like the latter all the pains and miseries of the body and has to remain incarnated there until it has managed to fulfill all its outstanding obligations. It then leaves the person. But when the impregnating soul enters a person because he needs its support, it does not suffer any of the pains and miseries of his body, as the helping soul is not itself deficient and has not arrived on its own behalf. Hence there is no set time before which it may not leave the body, but it dwells in the body for a longer or shorter period at its own discretion. If the person does what is good, it stays with him and unites with him more intimately the better he becomes; but if he does what is evil, it separates from him on its own authority."

WALKING ON WATER
(Chapter XLVIII)

Iamblichus says that when seers are impelled by the divinity, they fear nothing and shrink from nothing; they cross impassable places, throw themselves—without any harm worth mentioning—into the fire, and leap over rivers.

IAMBLICHUS (283–333) was a Neoplatonist who on one occasion experienced a divine influx or "Cosmic Consciousness." Apart from the time when the Lord walked on water (Matthew 14: 25 f.), we have similar reports concerning both Christian and non-Christian saints. I shall confine myself here to the Christian ones and, in particular, to Peter of Alcantara (1499–1562), the founder of the order of barefoot Franciscans. Jakob Joseph GÖRRES said of him, among other things, in his *Christlichen Mystik* [Christian Mysticism]: "They (the saint and his companions) entered the flood (of the swollen Guadiana) and crossed over. The water reached only to his ankles. . . . He made his way over the raging water as unconcerned as if he were on solid ground."[28] Dr. Wilhelm MOUFANG (born in 1895) from whose valuable book I have taken this short extract, also says, "It is hardly legitimate to dismiss a report of that kind with such cli-

---

[28] Joseph von Görres, *Mystik und Dämonie* [Mysticism and Demonism], Die christl. Mystik in Auswahl, edited by Joseph Bernhart, Munich, 1927.

chés as 'hallucination,' 'mass suggestion,' etc., even if Görres does report it uncritically."[29]

It may still be unknown to the majority of our readers that "in her younger years the poetess, Baroness Annette von DROSTE-HÜLSHOFF (1797–1848) was able to walk on water when she wanted to take a short cut to her ancestral Wasserburg."[30] She also possessed the fatal gift of the second sight (*deuteroscopy*), like two other Westphalian poets, her friend Levin SCHÜCKING (1814–1883) and Friedrich Wilhelm WEBER (1813–1894), the author of *Dreizehnlinden* [Thirteen Lime Trees].

OUT-OF-THE-BODY EXPERIENCES
(Chapter L)

According to the Histories of Herodotus, there lived in Proconnesus a wonderfully erudite philosopher named Atheus , whose spirit sometimes left his body and, after ranging far and wide, returned enriched with new knowledge. . . . Pliny relates the same thing of the soul of Harmon of Clazomenae, which also used to leave its body to wander freely and bring back many true reports from far afield. Even today one encounters many Norwegians and Laplanders who are able to separate themselves from their bodies for three days at a time and to return with much news from distant regions. . . . But during this time no live animal must come up and touch them, otherwise they will no longer be able to re-enter their bodies.

Pliny refers to this in his *Natural History* (VII; 52):

As regards the soul, we find quoted as a prodigy that the soul of the Clazomenian, Hermotimos, on leaving

---

[29] Dr. Wilhelm Moufang, *Magier, Mächte und Mysterien* [Magicians, Powers, and Miracles], Heidelberg, 1954, 231–232.
[30] Willy Schrödter, *Grenzw. Versuche* [Paranormal Research for All], 128, see chapter on "Levitation."

> *his body often rambled about and, after its travels, had much to say about events which could not have been observed except by someone who was present at them; while in the meantime his body is said to have been only half alive. In the end, his enemies, the Kantharider, burnt his body and so deprived the soul of its so-called sheath.*

Speaking of the astral journeys of the Lapps, we need mention only the classic case which AXEL, the (Protestant) archbishop of Uppsala witnessed in the presence of a senior official and a medical man regarding the wealthy Laplander Peter LÄRDAL, and prepared a circumstantial report on it.[31] That the touch of animals or humans can cause a fatal *choc de retour* to a cataleptic who is astral traveling is well known to the adepts; which is why those Indian yogis who practice the art will retire into caves for the duration of the *mayavirupa* as they term it, and they leave their chelas on guard over their physical casket. The number of well-attested cases in the serious literature on the subject is legion!

NEAR-DEATH EXPERIENCES
(Chapter L)

> *Since, according to the doctrine of the Egyptians, the soul is a spiritual light, it comprehends—when separated from its body—every place and every time; just as a light shut inside a lantern shines everywhere when the lantern is opened. Cicero remarks in his book on Divination that the human soul foresees the future only when it is so disengaged from the body that it has little or nothing to do with it. . . . That is to say, there dwells in our soul a universal clairvoyance which is hindered by the opaqueness of the body and by mortality; but after death, when the soul is liberated from the body, having become immortal, it attains to perfect*

---

[31] Enno Nielsen, *Das Große Geheimnis in Neuzeit und Gegenwart* [The Great Secret in Recent Times and Today], Ebenhausen bei München, 1923, 113.

knowledge. Therefore an unaccustomed light is quite often granted to those who are near death and weakened by old age, because since the soul is then less fettered by the senses and is already partly freed from their bonds, and is nearer to the place to which it is shortly going, and is no longer as subject to the body as formerly, it now sees more clearly and thus easily receives revelations in the final moments of life.

There is nothing much we need add to this: anyone who cares to make inquiries in their circle of friends and acquaintances will be able to gather sufficiently convincing information. They will also learn that long-term inmates of mental institutions often come to their senses just before their demise and that the medical profession, itself, regards this improvement as a sure sign of impending death.

PROPHETIC DREAMS
(Chapter LI)

The dreams I am talking about here are those that arise as a union of understanding and fantasy, either through the thought-processes acting on the soul or through a pure revelation imparted by some higher being, given the necessary purity and tranquillity of spirit. For it is only in such dreams that our soul produces genuine oracles that may be accepted as prophetic. In these dreams we seem to ask, to learn, to read, and to discover. What is more, much that is doubtful, unknown, unexpected, and unsought becomes patent to us in dreams of this kind. We see views of unknown places and the forms of individuals both living and dead; also things which have not yet happened or, if they have happened somewhere, are still unknown to us.

I should like to draw attention here to the remarkably interesting "didactic dreams" mentioned in the middle paragraph. As regards inventions (and discoveries) made in dreams, I have elsewhere published a collection of no less than twenty-five of them,[32] without being able to lay claim to completeness. Especially neat is the story of how the American industrialist Elias HOWE (1819–1867) discovered the principle of automatic threading for the sewing machine. He dreamt that knights were piercing the pointed ends of the needles with their lances, and that cords with pennants hanging on them were drawn through the holes they had made. This is the novelty of sewing-machine needles, that the eye is situated at the point and not at the blunt end as in ordinary sewing needles! Here is an example of a find made through a dream: the French consul BREST dreamt that he dug in a certain place on the island of Melos and unearthed a wonderful statue. When the dream came to him the third time, he actually made the dig and discovered the Venus de Milo, which is now in the Louvre in Paris. This happened in 1820.[33]

Of musical compositions that come in dreams, we need mention only the "Devil's trill" sonata given to Giuseppe TARTINI (1692-1770) in 1713.[34] And regarding the reading of books in dreams, a Renaissance scholar in Dijon was having trouble translating a Greek poet. In a dream he felt himself being transported to the Royal Library in Stockholm, where he turned to a certain section of a certain volume and found the verse translated there. Renatus CARTESIUS (René Descartes, 1596–1650), who was in Stockholm, confirmed that everything tallied perfectly.[35] Past master KIESEWETTER says of himself: "I, too, when I am asleep, peruse long passages in books that are unknown to me; and then, when I am reading something when I am awake, the memory comes back to me and I experience in a flash of realization that I have already dreamt it!"[36]

While we are still on the subject, two examples come to mind of what AGRIPPA says about being taught in dreams by

---

[32] Willy Schrödter, "Den Seinen gibts der Herr im Schlaf" [Divine Revelations in Sleep] in *Okkulte Stimme,* Part 6, Brunswick, June, 1958, 22–23.

[33] Jos. Ant. Maximilian Perty, *Die mystischen Erscheinungen der menschlichen Natur* [The Mystical Phenomena of Human Nature], Leipzig, 1861, II, 371.

[34] Wilhelm Moufang, *Mysterium der Träume* [The Mystery of Dreams], Munich, 1953, 76–77; Stege, 286–287.

[35] Dr. Carl du Prel, *Die Entdeckung der Seele durch die Geheimwissenschaften* [The Discovery of the Soul Through the Occult Sciences], Leipzig, 1895, II, 151.

[36] Carl Kiesewetter, *F. A. Mesmers Leben und Lehre* [F. A. Mesmer's Life and Teaching], Leipzig, 1893, 84.

"higher beings": the abbot TRITHEMIUS was taught his *Stegan-ographia* (1505) by just such an entity in 1499.[37] My friend, Dr. Adolf S. dreamt he was standing in a subterranean vault. In front of him was a long table, at which there were sitting about a dozen white-bearded old men wearing tall black pointed caps, the badge of a certain spiritual hierarchy. Behind him was a gigantic open bookcase containing many scrolls. One of the elders stood up solemnly, took one of the scrolls in his hand, unrolled it and read out (approximately): "What you wish your fellows to do to you, do to them! Bstanghygur Mdo . . . Tandschur Dö." A week later, by coincidence, the then Marburg student purchased an almanac of Buddhist sayings by SEIDENSTÜCKER. In one place there was exactly the same saying in exactly the same words out of the Tibetan Tandschur.

Hans BLÜHER (1888–1955), whom no one could accuse of being gullible, also admitted the reality of things read when one was asleep, and he considered the enigmatic texts seen in dreams to be "evidence of a former life."[38] Credible individuals have assured me that although they have not read any books on the other plane, full-length lectures are certainly given there. My obligation to respect the privacy of informants who are still living stops me from supplying further details. Finally, the opinion expressed by PARACELSUS on the subject of "creative dreams" deserves a mention here: "So, too, all practitioners have received many instructions and revelations in sleep and dreams when they were inflamed with a burning desire to have them. Their imagination has worked wonders upon wonders and has attracted to them a philosophical *Evestrum* ("spiritual shadow," or "astral body") which has imparted its skill to them. As a matter of fact, this happens quite often, but the majority of the communications are not remembered, for in the morning the sleeper wakes up and says, "I have had a wonderful dream last night: Mercury (or some other wise being) appeared to me and taught me this and that, but it has gone from me and I cannot remember

---

[37] Dr. Carl du Prel, *Die Magie als Naturwissenschaft* [Magic as Natural Science], Leipzig, 192, II, 245; Silbernagl, *Johannes Trithemius,* Regensburg, 1885, 98; Johs. Trithemius, *Polygraphia: Expositio Adolphi a Glauburg;* Carl Kiesewetter, *Faust,* 397.

[38] Hans Blüher, *Traktat über die Heilkunde* [A Treatise on Medical Science], 3rd. revised edition, Stuttgart, 1950, 42.

what I heard. Anyone who experiences something like this should not leave the bedroom on waking, nor speak to anyone, but should remain alone without eating until everything comes back and the dream is remembered."[39]

DREAMWORK
(Chapter LI)

(Therefore) whoever wishes to have prophetic dreams must be enjoying good physical health, his brain must not be fogged, and he must not be full of emotion; also he must go without supper on the day in question and must not drink anything intoxicating. His bedroom must be clean and neat, as well as being exorcised and consecrated; what is more, incense must be burned and his temples must be rubbed with ointment. Dream-inducing rings must be put on his fingers, a scheme of the heavens must be placed under his pillow, and he must go to bed calling on the Godhead with holy prayers and having his thoughts concentrated on what he desires to know. For then he will receive true and unambiguous dreams and their meaning will be disclosed to him.

A little further on (chapter LIII) we read:

Solomon received in a dream one night, a wisdom encompassing things above and things below. And in much the same way, Isaiah, Ezekiel, Daniel, and the other prophets and apostles have been instructed.

Depth of insight is displayed in a maxim inscribed shortly before the above sentence (chapter LIII):

---

[39] Dr. Franz Freudenberg, *Paracelsus und Fludd* [Paracelsus and Fludd], The "Geh. Wissenschaften" Series, No. 17, Berlin W. 30, 1918, 153. [Also, while keeping the eyes shut, one can try to recollect one small detail (word, action, person, place, thing, etc.), for once this "handle" has been grasped, so to speak, the door back into the dream may reopen. Tr.]

Now when the human soul has been duly purified and sanctified, it emerges to move freely unimpeded by any disturbing influences, elevates itself, perceives the divine, and actually instructs itself, even though it seems to have received its information from some other source.

I have given a historical sketch of "dream-work" in the section of that name in my *Grenzwissenschaftlichen Versuche* [Paranormal Research for All] and have shown elsewhere[40] what can be achieved by such *monoideism*. Here I shall do no more than point out that by this form of concentration contact can be made with the spiritual hierarchies known as "Rosicrucian." All the adepts agree on this, from Ägidius GUTMANN (1490–1584)[41] and Julius SPERBER (died in 1616)[42] through Edward George BULWER-LYTTON (1803–1873).[43] Among other things, our author prescribes the use of incense and of an ointment, which was no doubt scented. And, as it happens, a modern adept—the Berlin physician Dr. Friedrich SCHWAB (1878–1946)—was engaged in producing dreams to order. According to him, whatever one wishes to experience in a dream should be thought about vividly during the day while inhaling a given perfume slowly and deliberately, in order that one's thoughts are identified as much as possible with the aroma; then, on retiring, a few drops of the perfume are placed on the pillow, and it is extremely likely that the desired dream will occur during the night as the odor does its work.

Having absorbed the aroma when we were in the waking state, and having associated it with a certain idea, it will evoke

---

[40] Willy Schrödter, "Healing Suggestions in Dreams," in *Mensch & Schicksal,* No. 12, Villach, September 1, 1953, 17 f (see p. 265); and "Healing Herbs Revealed in Dreams," in *Pflanzen-Geheimnisse* [Plant Secrets], Warpke-Billerbeck, 1957, 202 f; "Ancestral Spirits Answer Us," in *Okkulte Stimme,* Part 23, Brunswick, December, 1952, 25 f; "Divine Revelations in Sleep: Inventions & Discoveries in Dreams," in *Okkulte Stimme,* No. 6, Brunswick, June, 1958, 22 f.

[41] Ägid. Gutmann, *Offenbarung Göttl: Majestät, etc.* [Revelation of the Divine Majesty, etc.], Frankfort-on-the-Main, 1619, L.VIII; Willy Schrödter, *Die Rosenkreuzer* [The Rosicrucians], Lorch/W., 1952, 28.

[42] Julius Sperber, *Echo der von Gott erleuchteten Fraternitet des löblichen Ordens Rosae Crucis, etc.* [An Echo of the Divinely Illuminated Fraternity of the Worshipful Order of the Rosy Cross, etc.], Danzig, 1615.

[43] E. G. Bulwer-Lytton, *Zanoni,* London, 1842.

the same idea when we encounter it again. The perfume should be chosen from astrological considerations, which it would take us too far afield to explain here.[44] What is more, in training children, one can give them suggestions coupled with certain aromas during the day, and can activate these suggestions during the night when they are asleep by placing near them a piece of cloth sprayed with the chosen scent.[45]

THE ORACLE OF OVERHEARD WORDS
(Chapter LII)

In Pharai, a city of Achaia, there once stood a statue of Mercury in the middle of the market, and anyone who wanted a sign would burn incense in front of it, light lamps, and place a local coin in the right hand of the image, and would whisper in its ear whatever he wanted to know. He then clapped his hands over his ears, rushed from the marketplace and, after he was out of it, he unblocked his ears and treated the first voice he heard as an omen and an oracle. Although to blockheads, who treat the outcome as pure chance, lotteries of this kind seem senseless, they are guided by God and the higher powers along certain lines and are not in conflict with the will of those who direct them.

When Saul was chosen by lot to be king of Israel,[46] did it not look fortuitous—and yet the Lord had already designated him as king[47] and the prophet Samuel had anointed him?[48] God, who had named him as king, guided the drawing of lots in his favor. And now I believe I have said everything that needs to be said on the matter.

---

[44] Dr. Frdr. Schwab, *Sternmächte und Mensch* [The Stellar Powers and Mankind], Zeulenroda, 1933.

[45] Dr. Arnold Krumm-Heller, *Osmologische Heilkunde* [Osmological Therapy], Berlin, 1955, 116; Dr. Ernst Busse, "Die Schlafbeflüsterung, eine unfehlbare Erziehungs-und Heilmethode" [Whispering to Sleepers, an Unfailing Method of Training and Cure], in *Okk. Stimme*, Part 7, Brunswick, July, 1955, 22 f.

[46] I Samuel 10: 20–21.

[47] I Samuel 9: 15–17.

[48] I Samuel 10: 1.

Earlier, the "demonic knight" (as ARAM calls him) had supplied details of the sacred preparations necessary for receiving "lots and signs that would count as oracles" and could be obtained only on specific occasions. The oracle of overheard snatches of conversation is as old as the human race and is extremely widespread. The Jews called it *Bath-qol* ("the daughter of a voice"),[49] the Chinese know it as "listening to the mirror,"[50] in the Middle Ages the Germans termed it "eavesdropping,"[51] and nowadays (in the Saxon Vogtland) it is referred to as "casting lots."[52]

In its written form, this type of divination is known as "Bibliomancy" (and also, but erroneously, as "stichomancy") and counts among its apologists GOETHE,[53] Friedrich LIENHARD (1865–1929),[54] and Hans BLÜHER (1888–1955).[55] Here are three specimens out of many: 1) In the "Elective Affinity" (1809; I: c. 12) of GOETHE (1749–1832), the captain of the Charlotte describes how easily the boat is steered by a person. "At these words, the girlfriend felt the imminent separation in her heart. 'Has he said this on purpose?' she wondered, 'Does he already know about it?' Has he guessed it, or has he said this accidentally, so that he foretells my fate unconsciously?" 2) The "miracle apostle" and "backwoods student," Hans STERNEDER was in two minds whether or not to leave his beloved Castellamare in the Gulf of Naples. The hours he spent tormenting himself over it can be seen as a sort of prayer. Then, as he was passing a cottage outside the place, he heard through the open door a girl saying to her sweetheart, "You must stay now." This gave the Austrian writer a start—and he stayed.[56] 3) Wilhelm von SCHOLZ (born 1874) had the following incident told to him: his

---

[49] Franz Freudenberg, *Der Blick in die Zukunft* [The Peep into the Future], Berlin, 1916, 16; [However, According to Alan Unterman, *Dictionary of Jewish Lore & Legend,* Thames & Hudson, London, 1991, 34, a *bat-kol* is a "heavenly voice which continued to communicate God's messages to man after biblical prophecy came to an end." This treats it as entirely supernatural and not involving overheard human speech. Tr. note.].

[50] Hwang Tsu-Yü, *Der blühende Granatapfelbaum* [The Flowering Pomegranate Tree], Munich, 1916, 16.

[51] Adolf Wuttke, *Der dt. Volksaberglaube der Gegenwart* [Popular Superstitions in Present-day Germany], Leipzig, 1925, 246–247 § 357.

[52] Wuttke, p. 238 § 341.

[53] J. W. v. Goethe, *West-Östlicher Divan.*

[54] Friedr. Lienhard, *Unter dem Rosenkreuz* [Among the Rosicrucians], Stuttgart, 1925, 168.

[55] Hans Blüher, *Werke und Tage* [Works and Days], Munich, 1953, 217 f.

[56] Hans Sterneder, *Sommer im Dorf* [Summer in the Village], Leipzig, 1931, 305 f.

informant was passing a (closed) linen-draper's shop, noticed nightclothes on display, and remembered that for some time he had been meaning to buy some. A long way from the shop, he had to pass a courting couple and heard the young man talking to the girl (she was "very pretty") about night attire. "I was quite struck by it, and sighed with old Faust: 'If only I could dismiss magic from my path'!" So ends this short report.[57]

As far as the phenomenon itself is concerned, we might add that: The Viennese baron and dietician, Dr. Ernst von FEUCHTERSLEBEN (1806–1849) offers the following advice: "Get up and go, with your sick, perplexed mind, with your doubts and fears, into the circle of human society; where a casual word has often illuminated, like a flash of lightning, the most dreadful night."[58] Martin BUBER (1878-1965) philosophized: "Life involves being addressed. We are immersed in a world of signals, but most of us stay in our shells, which makes us deaf to what they have to say." Eduard MAY maintains that, "The entire scene of world affairs is highly deterministic. There are no un-caused or acausal events; but each event is determined during its course by a complex of causes or conditions that for their part are determined, as to their very existence and nature, by causes or complexes of conditions lying further back—and so *ad infini-tum*." Emboldened by this support, I sum up: Since nothing, ab-solutely nothing, happens by chance, "every hair of our head is numbered," and if we take it literally, "one ... [sparrow] ... shall not fall on the ground without your Father" (Matthew 10: 29–30). Therefore the snatches of conversation we overhear from passersby may be treated as intentional omens or signs for us when we are in critical situations.

Probably one should not expect God to intervene through one of his messengers (Latin: *angeli* = angels). Subspecie *æternitatis,* that would be using a sledge-hammer to crack a nut, *sit venia verbo.*[59] Surely we must leave to HIM the type and meth-od of the revelation. Therefore (and in opposition to Agrippa!) I

---

[57] Wilh. v. Scholz, *Der Zufall u. das Schicksal* [Accident and Fate], Leipzig, 1942, 125.

[58] E. v. Feuchtersleben, *Zur Diätetik der Seele* [The Dietetics of the Mind], Halle/S, 1910, 148.

[59] ["If it is permissible to say so." The author is enjoying himself with some Latin tags here, which are worth leaving in to preserve the flavor of his book. Tr. note.]

do not think it would be proper to copy Abraham's servant (in Genesis 24) by proposing one's own sign. Even less should we take it upon ourselves to advise others to seek a sign when they are making a decision. On the other hand, we should certainly not shut our eyes to it when a sign unexpectedly forces itself on our attention.[60]

MUMMIFYING CAVES
(Chapter LXIV)

The offerings deposited beside the statue of Minerva in Troas did not decay.

A modern European example is the Bleikeller beneath Bremen cathedral, which "has the unusual property of preserving from corruption the bodies placed in it. A number of corpses, mostly of foreign and unknown people who died in Bremen hundreds of years ago, are lying in open coffins, and the bodies are well preserved although completely desiccated. The crypt still keeps its antiseptic power because the bodies of small creatures, such as dead chickens, sparrows, dogs, parrots, and rats, are similarly preserved."[61]

Other mummifying cellars, so my informant tells me, are to be found in the village of Arnim near Bremen, in a monastery on the Venusberg near Bonn, in the church crypt of the (former) Estonian seaport Hapsal, and the famous catacombs in Kiev. I have mentioned others elsewhere.[62] It is a pity that we are still unable to work out what gives these rooms their preservative properties: "otherwise, instead of the expensive refrigerating chambers and ice-houses, which do no more than slow down

---

[60] Willy Schrödter, "Das Orakel der aufgefangenen Worte" [The Oracle of Overheard Words] in *Neue Wissenschaft*, Part 4, Oberengstringen/Zürich, July/August, 1959, 165–170.

[61] Artur Moszkowski & Alex Fürst, *Das Buch der 1000 Wunder* [The Book of 1000 Wonders], Munich, 1916, 235 f (No. 173).

[62] Willy Schrödter, "Mumien" [Mummies] in *Das Geistige Reich*, Part 10/11, Grödig/Salzburg, October/November, 1960, 290–295.

putrefaction without stopping it, we could employ similar anti-septic cellars for preserving foodstuffs." If their secret were only known to us, muses Prof. Otto Nik. WITT (1853–1915) in *Narthekion* (1901), we might occasionally try the experiment of isolating patients suffering from infectious diseases in such rooms, as now we pack them off to the bacteria-free air of Davos, Heluan, or Lapland. Also it would be useful to study and em-ploy the antibiotic properties of the mold that thickly covers bodies as soon as one year after burial.[63]

Hans BLÜHER (1888-1955), without offering any expla-nation or investigating further, states that "there are places on earth that have uniquely determined fates: in some the sick be-come well, in others dead bodies do not decay."[64] Jörg Lanz von LIEBENFELS (1873-1954) was more specific: "It is an established fact, open to confirmation, that the earth has various regions with different radiations. The so-called mundane horoscope is based on this fact. Ancient religions, and even medieval Chris-tendom, were aware of this fact, and assigned each spot to a *ge-nius loci* (spirit of the place), which in Christian times came to be known as patron saints. Each saint is the hieroglyph or represen-tative of a special type of vibration, which can be interpreted as-trologically."[65]

Frenzolf SCHMID has determined experimentally that certain places and certain people have specific radiations. Some emit good (healing) rays, and others emit evil (death) rays. The patron saints indicate the nature of the radiations in the places assigned to them.[66] In this connection it should be noted that the mummification of small dead animals and of cut flowers can be effected by human magnetism radiated from the hands.[67] A prime example is that of the Nuremberg honorary professor, Heinrich NÜSSLEIN (1879–1947), who, in addition to practicing this "odic mummification," was also well known for his mediu-

---

[63] Schrödter, "Mumien," 290–295.

[64] Hans Blüher, *Traktat über die Heilkunde insbes. die Neurosenlehre* [A Therapeutic Treatise with Special Reference to the Neuroses], Stuttgart, 1950, 124.

[65] Jörg Lanz v. Liebenfels, *Bibliomystikon,* Vienna, 1932, IV, 152; Cf. the section on "the evil eye"!

[66] *Bibliomystikon,* Vienna, 1931, III, 65–66.

[67] Schrödter, *Grenzw. Versuche* [Paranormal Research for All], 155 f, chapter on "mum-mification," 175 f. and chapter on "odic conservation," *Präsenzwirkung,* 72, 218.

mistic dream paintings. From 1924 onward, this almost blind "picture scribe" was inspired to produce—in the incredibly short times of four through fifteen minutes, and even in pitch-darkness—not less than 20,000 "colored prayers" of considerable artistic merit.[68]

PRAYER PROMOTES PLANT GROWTH
(Chapter LXIV)

Also the turnip is said to grow bigger if, when it is sown, it is adjured to be serviceable to us, our families, and our neighbors.

"In 1952 in Los Angeles (CA) the "Religious Research Foundation" was set up, and the 45 year-old Franklin LOEHR, who was both a clergyman and a graduate chemist, was installed as its director. The aim of the Institute is to give scientific evidence of the power of prayer. With this intent, Loehr and his team of experts, encouraged by Prof. Joseph Banks RHINE (born in 1895) of Duke University in Durham, NC, have performed hundreds of experiments on plants and animals in recent years. Tests performed using controls have shown undeniably that:

1) Corn watered with water that has been prayed over grows better than corn watered with ordinary water;
2) Seed that has been prayed over grows better than seed that has not been prayed over;
3) Seed over which "negative prayers" have been said, expressing the wish that they would not thrive, do not grow as well as seeds which have not been prayed over.

---

[68] Franz Karl Fekl, "Heinrich Nüsslein, der okk. Maler von Nürnberg" [Heinrich Nüsslein, the Occult Painter of Nuremberg], in *Ztrbl. f. Okk.,* Leipzig, February, 1913, 372; Karl Schönenberger, *Legenden zu den 157 Bildern von Heinrich Nüsslein* [Explanations of the 157 Pictures of Heinrich Nüsslein], Zürich, 1946, 3–6; Heinr. Nüsslein, *Metaphysische Malerei* [Metaphysical Painting], Munich, 1949.

As far as the prayers themselves are concerned, it has been established that:

1) Praying out loud is more effective than praying mentally;[69]
2) Stretching out the hands in blessing over the plants increases the effectiveness of the prayers;
3) Visualization of the growth while praying for it also promotes it.[70] The great French esoteric publicist, Paul SEDIR (Yvon Leloup, 1871–1926) endeavored, in a whole chapter of his book on initiation,[71] to demonstrate the practical value of processing round fields. The Toba-Batak in Sumatra leave out in the sun for several days the seed-rice that has been soaked in water, "in order that its life-force can be enhanced by the rays of blessing. And, when they do this, they say to the rice: "Behold the sun, O our seed-rice, and grow!"[72]

---

[69] The Lord told his disciples (in Luke 11: 2): "When ye pray, *say* . . .," not, "When ye pray, *think*"!

[70] Willy Schrödter, *Grenzw. Vers.* [Paranormal Research for All], 220 f, chapter on "Seed-corn Grows as Commanded."

[71] Paul Sédir, *Initiations* (chapter on "La Vigne" [The Vine]), Biherol-les-Rouen, 1924, 139 f.

[72] Dr. Joh. Winkler, *Die Toba-Batak auf Sumatra in gesunden und kranken Tagen* [The Toba-Batak of Sumatra in Times of Sickness and Health], Stuttgart, 1925, 47.

CONCLUSION

But you, O sons of art and wisdom, search in this book and look for our scattered meaning, which we have supplied in various places,[73] for what we have concealed from you in one place we have revealed in another, in order that you may not be left wondering. . . . But no one should be angry with me for diffusing the facts of this science in many places; because I have hidden them on account of profane persons . . . to keep the truth hidden from the foolish while leaving it within easy reach of the wise.

WHAT GOOD ARE TORCHES, CANDLES,
OR SPECTACLES,
IF PEOPLE DO NOT
WANT TO SEE?

Tail-piece from the Amphitheatrum Sapientiae Aeternae, etc. *Hanau, 1609, Hannover, 1619, by the theosophist, alchemist, and physician, Heinrich Kuhnrath (ca. 1560–1605).*

---

[73] A similar admonition is found at the end of chapter LI on "Prophetic Dreams": "Whoever manages to piece together what I have dispersed throughout this book will easily become proficient in oracles and dreams."

INDEX

Willy Schrödter (1897–1971) was a businessman and also served as a councilor in the German government. He spent his mature years studying and researching serious esoteric subjects. His notes have proven to be invaluable references to those who have read his other books—*A Rosicrucian Notebook: The Secret Sciences Used by Members of the Order* and *History of Energy Transference: Exploring the Foundations of Modern Healing,* both published by Samuel Weiser.